Vegetarian recipes from South India

like mother makes

Madhuram Shankar

Published by

Aaranya Publishers Limited
25 Lenborough Close
Buckingham
MK18 1SE
www.aaranyapublishers.com

ISBN 978 0 9531827 1 8

First published in Great Britain: November 1997
Second edition: December 2010

Cover Photo by Jingqi Li

Preface to the second edition

Time has wrought many changes since the book's first publication in 1997; the author is no more and could not realise the (publishers') dream of a sequel to the book. But her legacy of caring and sharing lives on, and those who were privileged to experience her cooking continue to salute her whenever they re-create the flavours with the help of her book. The second edition is dedicated to giving her spirit and welcomes new readers to the feast.

- Editor
December, 2010

About the book - by an enthusiastic user

"Vegetarian Recipes from South India" is the staple in our shelf of cookbooks.

Its appeal lies in the simplicity and effectiveness of the recipes. They are recipes for dishes that perhaps a generation or two ago every householder would have known, at least the way their mothers made them. But over time, as the focus has shifted away from cooking, this basic knowledge seems to have been lost, and so for the likes of my husband and myself, who found ourselves far from home and longing for the taste of home food, this book proved to be a Godsend. We weren't looking for fancy dishes or gourmet meals, but good, old-fashioned, comfort food. And that is what we found.

The recipes are laid out in an easy, step-by-step manner, and the ingredients listed in order of use. One thing my husband in particular found extremely helpful, and unusual in a cookbook - as any novice chef would agree - was the precise measurement given even for an ingredient such as salt, rather than the more common "salt to taste". Another excellent feature is the suggested menu alongside many recipes, pointing one towards a recommended combination of dishes.

This is a book that has not been as widely available as we would have liked, for we have wanted to gift it to innumerable people! Our copy looks rather worn and tattered now - but we prefer to think of it as well-loved. Here's to the author, for enriching all our lives.

-Yeshwanti Balagopal, Nottingham, U.K.

Contents

Rasam

Side Vegetables

Chutneys

Pachidis (Raita)

Sweet Dishes

Introduction

What was originally intended as a sort of survival-kit of recipes for family members and friends living outside of India, has grown into a book. The credit or blame, as it may be, goes entirely to my children and sons-in-law.

There is an ancient Tamil quote of wisdom which goes: "Those who speak of it, have not seen (the Divine), those who have seen, do not speak." In the same way, it is difficult to make neat formulae out of something that is essentially experiential.

All the same, I hope that these recipes serve a dual purpose: to bring the familiar within reach of those who already know this culinary tradition, and to kindle an interest for the unfamiliar in those who have not been exposed to this part of the taste-world.

The term "taste-world" with respect to India needs qualification. There are as many cuisines in India as there are states and languages, in fact, as there are dialects, communities and sub-sects. Each region broadly determines its own way of cooking, depending upon its major crops and the spices available locally.

And then, of course, the endless variations within each region.

The recipes in this book are predominantly from the Tamil Nadu region, one I am most familiar with. They can be further localised to Tamil-Iyer households, Tanjore district, the Kaveri river-belt etc. That is to say, these dishes have their unique tastes and flavours as a result of their being based in a unique history and geography.

I must add here that the book is but a tiny sample of the vast collective repertoire of this region. It is likely that it opens up a new vista of Indian cooking for many of the non-Indian readers, as the South Indian cuisine is not a well- entrenched part of the restaurant culture even within India, let alone outside.

A word about the general approach to food and food-making in the tradition I belong to. What I have learnt is that cooking is a combination of *Suchi, Ruchi, Acharam* - of cleanliness, taste and discipline. When my children were growing up, I sometimes had a hard time explaining to their "rational" minds the somewhat archaic and seemingly arbitrary kitchen practices followed by my in-laws: strict separation of vessels containing cooked and uncooked food-items, not cooking before having had a bath, not eating without having offered some freshly cooked rice to the family-deity and having fed the crows - and a whole host of other do's and don'ts. Some practices might have got exaggerated on the way, but the underlying principles are hygiene, reverence, respect, gratitude, sharing.

That brings me to the cover picture. The picture shows Goddess Annapurni, the goddess of food and plenty. In the Hindu iconography, the goddess is worshipped in many different aspects: Saraswati for wisdom, Lakshmi for wealth, Parvati for prosperity, and Annapurni with a ladle in hand symbolises the feeding of humanity with the food and milk of knowledge. In *Annapurnashtaka*, an 8th century Sanskrit text of great beauty, Sankara extols the virtues of Annapurni. The set of ten verses is a description and benediction at once. The last verse goes:

"O Annapurni! Always whole and never depleted! O Sankara's life-strength! Grant me the alms that will lead me to desirelessness and wisdom."

It is to Her that I dedicate this book.

"Like mother makes" is by and large a truism that has so far been common to many parts of the world. Since the recipes in this book are traditional ones, they do come from a common pool that mothers have contributed to down the generations. The title refers to all those mothers, and I am greatly indebted to them.

- Madhuram Shankar

Thank you...

For all of us 'children' who have been associated with this book, it has been a labour of love.

The book has come into being thanks to the encouragement of the small but solid circle of admirers of Amma's cooking. A big thanks to Venkat, Mahi, Peter, Joedy, and all their friends for their discriminating taste!

Thanks are due to Sridhar and Joedy for the initial work with computerising the manuscript, Richard for initiation into the world of Desk Top, Paul for teaching a few tricks with the final form that evolved out of a long process of much trial and mostly errors, Rob for designing the cover and at the end of the trail, Mark and John, the best production team one could have hoped for.

Kudos to the feedback-team led by Uma and consisting of Anand, Anke, Geeta, Gina, Mahi, Poonam, Saumya, Shujaat and Vibha for trying out the dishes and asking for more.

Special thanks to Guha, Mahi, Vibha and Uma for pruning and polishing the texts with meticulous care, Mahi, Vibha and Peter for applying their expertise to the task of marketing and distribution, Joedy for pulling Pablo Neruda's poem out of his vast hat and Appa for the translation of some of the quotes.

Watching Duncan shoot the cover picture of Goddess

Annapurni was an experience; the patience, the play , the care and the attention that went into it are the very elements that make up the ingredients of good cooking. And a special thank you to all other friends for their words of encouragement and faith in the project.

It has been a great pleasure to edit this book and to co-ordinate the various strands going into the making of it. Thanks for this privilege must partly go to the stars and partly to my mother.

- Hem

Notes

Some of the recipe-titles may be unfamiliar to non-South Indians. The brief description that follows the titles in parentheses should give an idea of what is in store.

By and large, I have used English terms for all ingredients. The few exceptions are in Hindi, although the recipes stem from a Tamil-speaking region. This is because most of the Indian grocery stores in the US or U.K. use Hindi terms for the ingredients and spices.
The glossary of corresponding terms in English, Hindi and Tamil may serve as a ready reference.

Lentils:
It might be useful to consult the following brief description until you can tell the various forms of lentils apart:

Toordal (Red Gram): Yellow lentils, flat in shape, most commonly used (see recipes for *Dal, Sambar, Rasam*).

Masoor dal (red split lentils), which is more easily available, is a good substitute. It take less time to cook, but falls a little short as far as flavour goes.

Channa dal (Bengal gram): Brighter yellow in colour, rounder in shape, used in many of the seasonings (see also recipes for *Adai* and *Paruppu usili*).

Urad dal (Black Gram): White, same size and shape as red split lentils. An important ingredient for seasoning and vital for *Idlis* and *Dosais*.

Moong dal: Tiny, pale yellow lentils (see recipe for *Cabbage koottu*).

Notes...

Dahlia: Split, toasted chickpea without the husk (see recipe for coconut chutney).

Your local supermarket probably has most of the Indian **spices and ingredients**, but you are better off buying some of the items in an Indian or oriental grocery store:

Mustard seeds: Black, bigger seeds are preferable to the smaller, brown ones, as the latter tend to jump off the pan.

Red chili powder from Indian stores are more suited to Indian cooking than cayenne powder. The Indian variety is less pungent and provides more colour.

Hing or asafoetida: Just a pinch of it used in almost all gravy and side vegetables makes a big difference. Available only in Indian grocery stores.

Brown sugar, known as jaggery (gur in Hindi) in lump form; Indian grocery stores are a better bet for this. Some of the sweet preparations can be made with the dark brown sugar from supermarkets, but the taste is not the same.

Coconut: Even in the US or in UK, I used fresh coconut in preference to desiccated coconut. The difference is certainly obvious for the purists. But the desiccated variety, made from dry coconut, is admittedly a timesaver.

Pots and Pans

Most of the kitchen equipment and utensils available outside of India can be adapted quite well for Indian cooking. The following are specially helpful.

Notes...

Pressure cooker or electric rice cooker: You will find that cooking time (and your personal time for monitoring progress) for rice, dal or red kidney beans gets considerably reduced. Since both types of cooker come with two or three stacks, you will be cooking rice, lentils and perhaps some vegetables simultaneously.
As rice requires less cooking time, use cold water for the rice and hot water for the lentils. The ratio of rice/ lentils to water is normally 1: 2. (Note: If you are not using a pressure cooker, increase the ratio to 1: 3, monitor the temperature and see that the water does not boil over). Some recipes call for a deviation in the proportion; follow the instructions.

Idli stand: I have successfully improvised with an egg-poacher, but an *idli stand* is certainly a convenience. It normally comes in two or three tiers, so that you can make 8 to to 12 *idlis* at a time.

Thick iron pan for making *dosai*, although a nonstick frying pan is most effective and uses up less oil.

Wok: Thick, round-bottomed woks are more suited to Indian cooking than flat frying pans.

Mini wok: Round and hollow and about 4 1/2" in diameter; ideal for seasoning, as it contains the oil in a small surface area.

Coffee grinder: Most effective for dry-grinding Indian spices in small quantities. Keep one exclusively for this purpose, if possible.

Notes...

Some basic hints

Seasoning: A crucial step, quite often the final touch that makes or mars a dish. Mustard seeds are the main ingredient. Different dishes require different spices besides mustard seeds.

Keep a mini wok or a small saucepan with a lid just for this purpose. Heat the wok (or saucepan) on low heat with one teaspoon of ghee (or melted butter) or oil as called for in the recipe. Add specified amount of mustard seeds. As they begin to pop, cover it with a lid to prevent the seeds from jumping off the pan. Be careful not to burn seeds. Add to the prepared dish.

If the recipe calls for any other ingredients for seasoning - like urad dal, green chilies, cumin etc - **keep them handy.** Add them as soon as the mustard seeds start to pop and allow them (usually the dals) to get browned. The ingredients should neither be under-fried nor over-fried. All it requires is coordination and concentration. In case the ingredients get burnt due to oversight, it is better to discard and do the seasoning afresh.

Ghee: Clarified or melted butter, known as *ghee*, is used more often than butter in South Indian cooking. Since this cuisine is light and practically fat-free, the use of a little ghee is not an excessive indulgence. The ancient Indian science of medicine, *Ayurveda*, in fact recommends it highly. Seasoning done with a teaspoon of ghee enhances the taste and flavour of a dish, especially *Rasam* or *Sambar.*

Ghee can be made in small quantities and stored. No refrigeration is needed.

Notes...

Method: Take 1/2 lb .unsalted butter. In a heavy, medium - sized saucepan, heat butter over medium heat. When the butter has melted, allow it to simmer on low heat. When it is almost done, the milk solids will collect at the bottom. Stir once or twice when it is melting. The critical point is when the liquid is turning to a golden colour and the milk solids start to turn brown. Remove the pan from heat, allow the clear golden liquid to cool down and strain into a glass jar or ceramic container.

The brown milk solids can be used in soups or *Sambar*. Dishes cooked in the same pan will have a lot of flavour and taste.

It is the normal custom in South Indian households to sprinkle a teaspoon of *ghee* on top of steaming hot rice before adding *Sambar* or any other vegetable gravy.

Tamarind juice: Tamarind pulp to make 'real' tamarind juice is normally available only in Indian grocery stores. Some of the gourmet grocery stores with an international profile might also stock it.

Soak specified amount of the tamarind in warm water (quantity of water should be less than the final volume required) for 10 minutes, so that the pulp gets soft and can be squeezed. Press and squeeze the pulp in the water with your hand. Strain the extract into a bowl. Add a little more water, repeat the process to reach required volume of tamarind juice.

Tamarind paste that you get in containers of different sizes is, of course, a good short-cut.

Notes...

Yoghurt: As most of the yoghurt brands available are quite creamy, besides not tasting quite like yoghurt, you could try making it yourself.

Boil half-fat milk and allow to cool. When it is still warm, add 2 tbs sour yoghurt as starter and stir thoroughly. Drop a whole green chili into the milk to hasten the process of setting, and remove it once the yoghurt is set (it does not in any way make the yoghurt pungent). The starter-yoghurt can be store-bought. If so, make sure it is unflavoured. If it is a warm day, leave it covered in a convenient corner in the kitchen, making sure it does not get subjected to repeated variations in temperature (for instance, near the cooking range). It will take a day for the yoghurt to set.

In winter, you will have to try a few tricks, like wrapping up the bowl in a warm blanket, keeping it in the warmest part of the house, for example, the boiler room or near a radiator. Alternatively, pre-heat the oven to 250º for 5 minutes. Reduce to 100º and keep the prepared milk inside for four to six hours.

Abbreviations used:

tsp	teaspoon
tbs	tablespoon
c	cup

Glossary

English	Hindi	Tamil
Almond	Badam	Badam paruppu
Asafoetida	Hing	Perungayam
Bengal Gram	Channa dal	Kadalai Paruppu
Black gram	Urad dal	Uluttam paruppu
Black pepper	Kaali miri	Milagu
Cardamom	Ilaichi	Elakkai
Cashew nuts	Kaaju	Mundiri
Chickpea flour	Besan	Kadalai mavu
Chili	Mirchi	Milagai
Coriander seeds	Dania	Kottamalli virai
Coriander leaves	Kothmeer	Pachai Kottamalli
Cumin	Jeera	Jeeragam
Curry leaves	Curry patta	Kariveppilai
Fenugreek	Methi	Vendayam
Ginger	Adhrak	Inji
Jaggery	Gur	Vellam
Mint	Pudina	Podina
Mustard seeds	Rai	Kadugu
Moong dal	Moong dal	Payattam paruppu
Puffed rice	Poha	Aval
Red gram	Tur dal	Tuvaram paruppu
Saffron	Kesar	Kesari
Semolina	Rava	Ravai
Sugar	Sakkar	Sakkarai
Tamarind	Imli	Puli
Toasted channa	Dahlia	Pottukkadalai
Turmeric powder	Haldi	Manjal podi
Wheat	Gehu (Aatah)	Godumai

Rice Dishes

"Like a heap of jasmine flowers" is the ultimate compliment for plain, white rice, when cooked just right.

Being the staple diet in South India, it forms the base on which the simplest and the most elaborate compositions of a meal are constructed.

The everyday fare, for example, could be
rice - a vegetable gravy - a side vegetable in the first round;
rice - rasam - side vegetable in the second,
rice - yoghurt - pickle in the final.

Any chutney, papad or salad that is served in addition is part of any or all the "courses". Besides, there is no strict sequence of 'courses' as in the western sense. For instance, it is not uncommon to mix the vegetables and sauces with the yoghurt when you come to the *grande finale*. It is literally a celebration in the round!

It is quite normal to serve 4 to 5 different rice dishes for a wedding feast or any other special occasion. The stress would obviously be on the different flavours rather than on quantity.

R i c e

"The Anicham flower withers when smelt;
but a mere cold look is enough to wither a guest."
- Tirukkural, chapter on Hospitality

Coconut Rice

Ingredients	Method
1 c rice	Cook rice and keep aside. (see Notes on page 10)
2 tbs oil 2 tbs ghee	♦ Heat oil and ghee in a skillet.
1 tsp mustard seeds 4 tsp urad dal 1 tsp channa dal 2 tbs chopped cashew pieces 3 small red chilies, finely chopped 2 small green chilies, finely chopped	♦ Pop mustard seeds on medium heat (see Notes on page 11). Add dals, cashews and chilies. (It may be wise to fry the cashews separately, as their frying time might vary depending on their quality, source, etc.) ♦ Fry ingredients on low heat until browned.
1 1/2 c shredded coconut 1 - 1 1/2 tsp salt 1/4 tsp hing A few curry leaves	♦ Add shredded coconut, salt, hing and curry leaves. ♦ Keep stirring over low heat until the coconut turns a light brown. Take care that the mixture does not get over-fried. ♦ Mix together with cooked rice. The ratio of rice to coconut mixture is a matter of preference and taste. Add 1-2 tsp ghee when mixing.

Comment On festive occasions, this is served as one of two or three differently flavoured rice dishes; The coconut mixture can be stored in a refrigerator for a week.

Tayir Sadam

(Rice with yoghurt and spices)

Ingredients	Method
1 c basmati rice	Cook rice and keep aside. (see Notes on page 10)
1/2 tsp salt 1 c milk	♦ While the rice is still lukewarm, add salt and milk; mix well. Let the mixture stand for about 10 minutes.
1 tbs ghee 1 tsp mustard seeds 1 tsp fresh, grated ginger 2 green chilies, finely chopped	♦ While the rice is cooling, heat ghee in a skillet; add mustard seeds, chilies and ginger.
A pinch of hing 2 c thick yoghurt A few sprigs of curry leaves	♦ Once the seeds pop and the ingredients are slightly browned, add hing. Remove from heat after 2 seconds, and add the mixture to the rice along with yoghurt and curry leaves. Stir together and serve.

Comment: Usually served as the last item in South Indian meals - along with pickles. Pay attention to the consistency before serving. As the rice cools, the yoghurt will get absorbed, leaving the dish drier than the desired level. Mix in a little more yoghurt before serving.

Lemon Rice

Ingredients	Method
1 1/2 c rice	Cook rice and set aside. (see Notes on page 10)
3 to 4 tbs lemon juice 1tsp salt 1/2 tsp turmeric	♦ Squeeze lemons into a bowl to make up 3 - 4 tbs juice; add salt and turmeric.
3 tbs oil 1 tsp mustard seeds	♦ Heat oil in a skillet and add mustard seeds.
2 tsp channa dal 2 tbs cashew pieces 1/8 tsp hing 2 - 3 green chilies, finely chopped	♦ As the seeds crackle, add channa dal, cashew pieces, green chilies and hing, and stir until the dals turn brown.
1 tbs fresh coriander (cilantro) chopped	♦ Mix with the lemon juice. Add chopped coriander. Stir well.
Comment: Lemon juice should not be directly heated. The lemon juice mixture can be stored in a refrigerator and used later.	♦ In a serving bowl, mix 3/4 of the cooked rice and 3/4 of the lemon juice mixture. Blend well. If the mixed rice is too tangy for your taste, add some more of the cooked rice. If it is too bland, add some more of the lemon juice.

Mustard Rice

Ingredients	Method
1 c rice	Cook rice and set aside. (see Notes on page 10)
Ingredients to be ground 3 small red chilies, finely chopped 1/2 tsp salt A pinch of hing 1/2 tsp turmeric A few curry leaves A marble-sized chunk tamarind	♦ Using very little water, grind ingredients listed alongside in a processor.
1 tbs ghee 1 tbs mustard seeds 1/4 c peanuts (unsalted) 1 tsp urad dal 1 tsp channa dal	♦ In a skillet, heat ghee and add ingredients listed alongside. ♦ Once the seeds start to crackle, add the ground ingredients and continue frying until the raw smell disappears and the masala and nuts turn brown. ♦ Mix with cooked rice and serve.

Sesame Rice

Ingredients	Method
1 c rice	Cook rice and set aside. (see Notes on page 10)
1/2 c white sesame seeds 3 small red chilies, chopped	♦ In a warm skillet, dry-roast sesame seeds and red chillies on low heat until seeds begin to crackle. Remove from heat.
1/2 tsp salt A pinch of hing	♦ In a processor or blender, grind the roasted sesame seeds, chilies, hing and salt to a powder.
2 tsp oil 2 tsp ghee 1 tsp mustard seeds 1 tsp urad dal 1 tsp channa dal A few curry leaves	♦ In a skillet, heat oil and ghee and add mustard seeds, dals and curry leaves. Fry until the dals turn brown. ♦ Blend this seasoning as well as the powdered mix with cooked rice and serve.

Comment Papads, chips or crisp stir-fried vegetables go well with this dish.
The sesame powder can be stored for later use.

Puliyodarai

(Tamarind Rice)

Ingredients	Method
1 c rice	Cook rice. Allow to cool (see Notes on page 10).
Lemon-sized chunk of tamarind pulp or 3 tsp tamarind paste dissolved in 1 1/2 c warm water 2 tsp salt 1 tsp turmeric 1/2 tsp hing 2 tsp brown sugar or jaggery	♦ Extract 1 1/2 c concentrated tamarind juice from pulp or by mixing paste with water (see Notes on page 12). Pour into a thick-bottomed saucepan, and add salt, turmeric, hing and jaggery. Boil mixture on medium heat until it is reduced to half the volume. Stir occasionally to prevent mixture from sticking to the pan . Reduce heat.
Ingredients to be powdered 1 tbs toor dal 1 tbs sesame seeds 1/4 tsp fenugreek	♦ While the gravy is cooking, dry-roast ingredients listed alongside, and powder in a blender. Add to the gravy. Stir to prevent lumps.
4 tbs oil 1 tsp mustard seeds	♦ In a skillet, heat oil and pop mustard seeds.

Puliyodarai - contd.

2 tbs channa dal 8-10 small red chilies 1 tbs unsalted peanuts A few curry leaves 1 tbs toasted sesame oil	♦ Add channa dal, red chillies, peanuts and curry leaves. ♦ When browned, add to the thickening tamarind gravy. On low heat, stir the gravy continuously until it is well-blended and thickens further. The oil will begin to gather on top, signalling the end of the process. Remove from heat and allow to cool. ♦ Mix desired quantity with the rice. Do not mix all the rice and sauce at once, but keep some back to work out the right balance. While mixing, add 2 tsp sesame oil.

Comment The sauce keeps for a long time.
A favourite dish in South India to take along on picnics.
Papads, chips or crispy stir-fried vegetables go well with this dish.
Advisable to finish with plain yoghurt or any of the *raitas*.
It can also be used as a thin spread over toasts.

Bissi Bela Hooli Anna

To make the powdered masala

2 tbs coriander seeds
2 tbs channa dal
1/8 tsp fenugreek seeds
3-4 black peppercorns
5-6 red chilies
1/4 cup fresh (unsweetened) shredded coconut
1 tbs butter

For the Bissi Bela

1 c rice
2 c water (to cook rice)
1/2 c toordal
1 c water (to cook dal)

Except for the coconut, fry all other ingredients in butter or ghee to a golden brown colour.

- Grind to a powder.
- Over low heat in the same pan, but without additional butter, fry the coconut to a light brown colour and powder. Mix the two together and give it a spin. Set aside.
- Cook rice and dal in separae containers in a pressure cooker (see Notes on page 10) to a very soft consistency. (If not using a pressure cooker, increase cooking time. Also add 1/ 2 c or more of water towards the end of cooking to arrive at a soft consistency).

Bissi Bela Hooli Anna - contd.

Ingredients	Method
2 1/2 tsp tamarind paste, dissolved in 1 1/2 c hot water 2 tsp salt 1/2 tsp turmeric	♦ Mash the cooked rice and dal together in a heavy-bottomed pan. Add salt, turmeric and tamarind water, and simmer on low heat for 10 minutes. ♦ Add the ground masala and stir well for 3 minutes.
1 tsp hing 2-3 curry leaves 3 tbs cashew nuts (unsalted) 3 tbs ghee 3 tbs oil	♦ Add hing and curry leaves, and simmer for half a minute. In ghee-oil mixture, quickly saute the cashews and add as garnish. Serve immediately, as the dish tends to solidify when cooled.
Suggested composition *Rasam* *Bissi Bela Huli Anna* Stir fried vegetable of choice Carrot salad Papads *Raita*	**Note:** The reason for frying and grinding the shredded coconut separately rather than *with* the rest of the ingredients is because fried coconut lets out oil, preventing the other ingredients from getting ground well.

Venpongal

(Spiced rice and lentils blended with milk)

1/4 c moong dal	In a skillet dry-roast moong dal on low heat for 5 minutes until the raw smell disappears.
1 c rice 2 1/2 c water	♦ Combine dal with rice and rinse. ♦ Pressure cook the rice and dal **together** with 2 1/2 c water to a soft consistency. This can be achieved by cooking for 10 minutes longer than normal on low heat. (If not using a pressure cooker, increase the quantity of water by 1 c).
1 tsp salt (more to taste) 1 c milk	♦ Mash the cooked mixture with a spoon, adding salt and milk.
2 tbs oil 3 tbs ghee 1/2 tsp ginger, chopped 2 tsp green chilies, chopped	♦ In a skillet, heat ghee and oil. ♦ Add chopped ginger, green chilies and cashews.

Ven Pongal - contd.

2 tsp cashews 1 tsp cumin seed 1/2 tsp ground black pepper A few curry leaves	♦ When the cashews begin to brown, add cumin, ground black pepper and curry leaves. Saute for a few seconds. ♦ Slowly add the mashed mixture and stir over low heat until well blended. ♦ Add a tsp of ghee individually when serving. ♦ The final consistency will be rather like that of Italian risotto.

Comment: May be served with *coconut chutney* and *eggplant gotsu* or *aviyal*. Looks equally good on the breakfast, lunch or dinner table!

Pongal denotes the act of boiling over of the rice and lentils. The prefix "Ven" means white - to distinguish it from other varieties of *pongal*. It is a must on the occasion of the Pongal festival, a thanksgiving celebration to mark the harvest season, when *Venpongal* and *Sakkarai pongal* (a sweet variety) along with sugarcane are offered to the deity.

Tomato Rice

Ingredients	Method
1 c rice	Cook rice and allow to cool. (see Notes on page 10)
4 c red tomatoes (chopped)	♦ Beat tomatoes in a blender. Do not strain; set aside.
<u>Ingredients to be fried and powdered</u> 2 tsp oil 4 dry, red chilies, finely chopped 3 tbs channa dal 1 tsp urad dal 1/4 tsp fenugreek 1/2 tsp hing 2 tsp shredded coconut 2 tsp coriander seeds	♦ In a skillet, fry all ingredients listed alongside until they release a pleasing aroma and the dals and seeds turn brown. ♦ Grind in a processor to a powder and set aside.
1 tbs oil 3/4 tsp salt 1/2 tsp turmeric	♦ Heat oil in a pan; add ground tomatoes, salt and turmeric. Simmer for 5 minutes.

Tomato Rice - contd.

Ingredients	Method
1 tsp sugar	♦ Add powdered ingredients to the tomato juice and mix well. Add sugar. Simmer until the juice thickens and oil begins to float on top.
2 tsp oil 2 tsp ghee 1 tsp mustard seeds	♦ In a separate skillet, heat oil and ghee; pop mustard seeds.
2 c onions, finely chopped 2 green chilies, finely chopped	♦ Add chilies and chopped onions, and fry to a golden brown. Add the cooled rice and mix well. ♦ Remove from heat; add the tomato concentrate and mix well. ♦ Mix with rice and serve.

Breads

Although South India is not the home of Indian breads, some varieties have been assimilated into the South Indian kitchens since a few generations.

Quite a few south Indian families opt for light *chappatis* in place of rice for the evening meal. Dry vegetables rolled into *chappatis* also make an easy packed lunch.

Parathas are a little heavier, as they are cooked in a bit of ghee or melted butter. Nevertheless, any one of the mixed vegetable gravies and two or three hot*parathas* is certainly a luxury to be indulged in occasionally. For *alu paratha* (*paratha* with a filling of potato), another superb invention, consult a good book on north Indian recipes.

Pooris, although deep fried, are so fluffy and light that they disappear faster than you can make them. The semi-liquid potato-onion mix as accompaniment is an absolute must. To have *pooris* without it is like eating pancakes without the maple syrup.

"Who hosts his guests with all his heart
and waits for more, will be hosted by the Gods."
- Tirukkural, chapter on Hospitality -

Breads

Paratha

Chappati

Poori

"Where is the need for him to sow and till, who puts the needs of his guests above his own?"
- Tirukkural, chapter on Hospitality

Paratha

2 c wheat flour (Aatah)
1/2 tsp salt
1/2 c water

In a shallow bowl, place the flour and salt and start mixing. Knead the mixture, adding water little by little to make a stiff dough. Keep aside for an hour.

Melted ghee

- Keep ghee in a liquid consistency ready at hand.
- Prepare about 15 small balls out of the dough. Roll out one to form a circle of 6 " diameter.
- Smear 1/2 tsp liquid ghee on the rolled paratha. Fold into half and fold over again to form a triangular shape. Roll it out into a larger triangle.
- Heat a nonstick skillet and place the paratha on it. Turn over when small bubbles form on the surface.
- Add 1 tsp melted ghee around the paratha. Rotate the paratha around on the skillet for the ghee to coat the entire surface.
- Turn over, add a little ghee and rotate around on the skillet. Remove when both sides are a golden brown.
- Repeat the procedure. Keep in an insulated, deep container.

Note : Goes well with *Potatoes and Peas Koottu*, *Peas Koottu* or *Vegetable Masala Koottu*. Any of the chutneys will be a fine addition.

Chappati

Ingredients	Method
1 c wheat flour (aatah) 1 tsp oil	In a deep bowl, mix flour and oil by hand.
1/4 c water 1/2 tsp salt	♦ Mix in salt and add water slowly. Keep kneading to form a soft dough. ♦ Cover and set aside for half an hour. ♦ Prepare 10 -12 small balls out of the dough. If you feel that the dough is too soft or moist, add a little flour and knead together.
1/2 c wheat flour in a separate bowl	♦ Take each prepared ball, knead, re-form and flatten between your palms, cover with dry wheat flour and roll with a rolling pin on a wooden board or marble to form a circle 6" in diameter. ♦ Heat iron or nonstick skillet over medium heat; transfer the rolled chappati on to the skillet. ♦ Turn it over when you see small bubbles forming. ♦ Keep rotating the chappati on

Chappati - contd.

the skillet with your hand or with a napkin for half a minute.

- Transfer it to open flame, if using a gas cooking range. It should puff up like a balloon. Remove into a deep dish.

5 tsp ghee

- Repeat the procedure. After every three or four chappatis, smear a little ghee on one side. Keeping the chappatis wrapped in a light, soft cloth will help to retain the softness.

Note: The critical factors are the following:

- the dough should be soft
- the chappatis should be evenly rolled
- constant attention should be paid that the skillet does not get over-heated.

Hot *chappatis*, *dal* and spiced vegetables make an ideal combination for a light evening meal.

Poori

Ingredients	Method
1 c wheat flour (Aatah) 1 tbs cream of wheat (Rava) 1/4 c water	In a shallow pan, mix wheat flour and rava together, adding water slowly to make a stiff dough. ♦ **Prepare this just 15 minutes before making the *pooris*.** ♦ Knead again and divide the dough into 8-10 balls. Roll each ball into a round shape of not more than 2" diameter.
Oil for frying	♦ Heat oil in a deep skillet or wok on medium heat. ♦ Slide each *poori* into the hot oil. ♦ As it starts puffing up, turn over. Remove with a slotted spoon to drain off oil and place in a shallow dish. ♦ Serve with potato-onion fry.

Light Meals

At one time in South India the dishes in this section (and many more) used to come under the heading of 'tiffin', a light interlude between early lunch (no breakfast) and dinner, consisting of something savoury and something sweet along with afternoon coffee. With changing workaday routines and eating patterns, this is now by and large reserved as a luxury for the odd weekend. The term 'tiffin' itself along with the practice is somewhat of a fading memory.

Thankfully, however, the dishes themselves have not fallen prey to changing eating habits; they have recast themselves as a special meal in place of what one would otherwise have for dinner.

There are some items - like the ubiquitous *idlis* - which pop up at any time of the day, some that are a complete meal by themselves and some that are more of an embellishment. And finally, for every dish that has been described here, there are five or more that have not found their way into this book, so great is the variety.

Light Meals

Idli

Ingredients	Method
2 c rice 3/4 c urad dal 1 tsp salt	Wash rice and urad dal separately. Soak them separately for 2 hours. ♦ Drain water from the rice and puree grind it, adding just a little water every two or three spins. Grind to a somewhat grainy consistency. ♦ Wash urad dal and grind to a very smooth consistency. Add water little by little after a few spins. The final consistency should be that of cake batter, neither too thick nor too runny. ♦ Add this to the ground rice dough and add salt. Mix well with a ladle or big spoon. Store in a warm place in a covered, deep container. The batter should ferment and rise by the next day. ♦ Steam the batter in a specially designed idli-stand (rather like an egg- poacher) which comes in two or more tiers of pans and is available in most Indian grocery stores. Smear the pans with oil before pouring in the batter.

Idli - contd.

- **Steaming**: Steam the idlis by placing the stand in a deep vessel with about an inch of water at the bottom. If using a pressure cooker, do not put the weight on to the lid. Once steam starts coming out forcefully, wait for 7-8 minutes before opening the lid. Remove the idlis carefully with a blunt knife.

- Serve with *sambar,* coconut chutney and *milagai podi* mixed with ghee in separate bowls.

Comment: If making several batches of idlis, be sure to replenish the water for steaming in between batches.

Note: You can reduce grinding time by using coarse cream of rice instead of rice. The proportions: 2 c cream of rice to 1 c urad dal. Mix just enough water with cream of rice to make a stiff dough. Grind to a semi-smooth consistency and mix with ground urad dal.

Semolina (Rava) Idli

Ingredients	Method
2 tsp oil 2 tsp ghee 1 tsp mustard seeds	In skillet, heat oil and ghee, and pop mustard seeds.
2 tsp urad dal 2 small green chilies, finely chopped 2 tbs chopped cashew nuts 1/4 tsp ground black pepper A few curry leaves	♦ Add ingredients listed alongside and saute.
1 c rava (also called semolina or cream of wheat) 3/4 tsp salt	♦ Once the dal turns brown, add rava and salt and keep stirring over low heat until the raw smell disappears and the rava turns a pale brown colour. Do not over-fry the rava.
2 c yoghurt A pinch of baking soda	♦ In a big pan, mix the fried rava with yoghurt. Stir together. Add baking soda and mix well. Let stand for 10 minutes.

Semolina (Rava) Idli - contd.

- Grease the idli mould with oil, pour the batter and steam, following the method outlined for rice *idli* (see page 40). As the consistency of this batter is thicker than that of rice *idli*, pour a little less of it into the moulds.
- Serve with chutney, sambar or gotsu.

Note: It is advisable to mix the prepared rava and yoghurt in two batches rather than a single large batch.

Comment: White steaming *idlis* served on green banana leaves are a feast for the eyes as well as the palate.
Idli has the knack of being just the right thing at any time - an energising breakfast, a quick bite at lunch, a light meal at night or a substantial Sunday brunch!

Sada Dosai

Ingredients	Method
1 c long-grained white or basmati rice	Soak rice and urad dal separately in a little over twice the quantity of water for a maximum of 2 hours. ♦ Drain rice and grind to a smooth paste, adding water little at a time.
1/2 c urad dal Water for the batter 1 tsp salt	♦ Wash the urad dal well three or four times, drain and grind to a smooth, thick paste, adding water little at a time. ♦ Add salt and mix the two batters together; store overnight in a warm place and allow to ferment. Leave enough room in the top of the container for the batter to expand (4-5" from the top) **The batter for this is prepared the same way as for idli (see page 40). The difference is that the rice should be ground to a smooth paste, so that the dosais turn out crisp.**

Sada Dosai - contd.

Oil or ghee for frying

Useful hint: Keep the spatula dipped in a container of water. The wet spatula helps ease the dosai off the pan.

- Heat skillet, smear oil or ghee and spread the dough like pancake batter, 6-8" in diameter.
- Sprinkle oil all around batter.
- Turn dosai over when the edges start crisping; add a little more oil or ghee if it threatens to stick to the skillet. Keep on skillet until golden brown, adjusting heat as necessary to prevent burning.
- This may be served with *chutney/ sambar/ milagai podi*, mixed with sesame oil or ghee.

Comment This extraordinary dish is unjustifiably called *Sada Dosai* or ordinary dosai, but only in order to distinguish it from variations like *oothappam* or *masala dosai*.

Note Once batter ferments, it is advisable to keep it refrigerated. In that case, leave it at room temperature for nearly an hour before preparing *dosais*, as very cold batter sticks to the skillet.

Masala Dosai

(Dosai with potato filling)

Ingredients	Method
	Prepare *dosai* batter as outlined in *Sada Dosai*. As the *dosais* should be very thin and crisp for this preparation, add a little more water for a thin consistency.
For the masala 4 medium potatoes, quartered	♦ Boil and peel potatoes and mash coarsely.
4 tbs oil 1/2 tsp mustard seeds 2-3 medium onions, diced 3 green chilies, diced	♦ Heat oil in a skillet and pop mustard seeds; saute green chilies and onion.
A pinch of turmeric 1 1/2 tsp salt 5-6 curry leaves A few sprigs of coriander	♦ Add turmeric, mashed potatoes, salt, curry leaves and coriander, and mix well. Remove from heat after 5 minutes.

Masala Dosai - contd.

Comment:

Two or three *masala dosais* with *sambar* and *chutney* is a filling meal, to be rounded off with either yoghurt or a sweet dish - or, of course, both!

To make the Dosai:

- To a well-heated, large, flat pan (preferably nonstick), add 1/2 tsp oil.
- Pour a ladle of *dosai* batter on to the pan in the middle and spread it concentrically to form a thin circle 9-10" in diameter.
- Add 1 tsp ghee or a mixture of ghee and oil around the circle of batter.
- Turn *dosai* over when it is a light golden brown and the edges start crisping.
- After a minute or so, turn it over once again and spread 2 tbs masala on one half of the circle. Fold over. Remove after 1-2 minutes, spreading a little ghee on top for added flavour.
- Serve with your favourite *chutney* or *sambar*.

Oothappam

(Dosai made from sour batter)

Ingredients	Method
	Prepare the *dosai* batter as outlined for *Sada Dosai*. Oothappam is made with three-day old, sour *dosai* batter and spiced up with onion, chili, etc.
2 tbs ghee or oil 2 medium onions, diced 2 bell peppers, chopped fine 2 green chilies, seeded and minced	♦ In a heated skillet, saute onion, green chilies and bell pepper in ghee or oil and set aside.
1/4 tsp fresh ground black pepper 1" piece ginger, grated	♦ Add black pepper and ginger to the batter and mix well.
Oil for frying	♦ Pour a ladle of batter on a heated skillet, spread it to form a circle and sprinkle oil around. Same procedure as for *Sada Dosai/ Masala Dosai*.

Oothappam - contd.

Note, however, that the *oothappam* is prepared thicker than *Sada Dosai*. The ideal thickness is about 1/4" minimum in the middle, and about 6'' in diameter.

- Turn *oothappam* over and spread onion-pepper mixture on top. Continue to cook for about 3 minutes and serve hot with coconut *chutney* or *sambar*, or both.

Note: The ideal *oothappam* is crunchy at the edges, golden brown on the outside, spongy on the inside.

Wheat Dosai

Ingredients	Method
1/2 c wheat flour 1/2 c rice flour 1/4 c plain flour	Mix wheat, rice and plain (*not* self-rising) flours together.
1/2 c yoghurt 1 c water 1 tsp salt 1/2 tsp cumin seeds	♦ Add water to yoghurt and beat together; mix with the flour mixture along with salt and cumin. Make sure there are no lumps.
2 small green chilies, finely chopped	♦ Add green chilies. ♦ Heat a nonstick skillet over medium heat, adding 1/2 tsp oil.
Oil for frying	♦ Pour a big ladle of batter in the middle of the skillet, spread thinly to form a circle. ♦ Add 1/2 tsp oil around the *dosai*. After a minute or two, turn it over. Sprinkle a little more oil or ghee for a crispier *dosai*. ♦ Serve with coconut *chutney* or *sambar*.

Note: This is a recipe to satisfy a sudden urge for *dosai*, as it does not involve a long preparation time. Instead of rice flour, you can use 1/2 c cream of rice. Grind to a smooth consistency with 2 tbs shredded coconut for enhanced flavour. Follow the rest of the steps in this recipe.

Semolina Dosai

1/2 c semolina
1/2 c buttermilk

1/2 c rice flour
1/2 c plain flour (not self-rising flour)
1/4 c wheat flour
1 - 1 1/2 tsp salt
2 green chilies, finely chopped
1/2 tsp cumin
1/2 tsp ginger, minced
1 1/2 c water (more if needed)
Ghee or oil for frying dosais

Soak semolina in buttermilk for 3 - 4 hours.

- Prepare dough by adding all the ingredients listed alongside to the semolina; mix thoroughly, making sure there are no lumps.
- Use a nonstick skillet for making the *dosai*. As the dough is **thin**, the method of applying the batter on the pan differs from other varieties of *dosai*. See Note below.
- After spreading batter on the pan, sprinkle 1-2 tsp oil around it and on top.
- When the edges start browning, lift gently and turn over. Remove after 2 minutes.
- Adding a tsp or two of ghee (instead of oil) makes the dosai crispier and adds to the flavour. Serve with coconut *chutney* and *sambar*.

Note: This batter has a tendency to 'set' as soon as it touches the skillet and hence cannot be spread around. Scatter the batter around the skillet in a quick motion, then fill in the gaps with more batter.
Practice makes perfect!

Aval Upuma

(Puffed Rice Upuma)

Ingredients	Method
1- 1 1/2 c puffed rice (Poha)	Wash puffed rice well and soak in water for 10 minutes. Squeeze out the water and set aside.
4 tsp oil 1 tsp ghee 1 tsp mustard seeds 1 tsp urad dal 1 tsp channa dal 1 green chili, cut small 1 dry, red chili, cut small	♦ Heat oil and ghee in a skillet over medium heat; pop mustard seeds. ♦ Add urad dal, channa dal and chilies.
1 tsp salt A pinch of turmeric 3-4 curry leaves A pinch of hing A few sprigs of coriander	♦ When the dals start to brown, add salt, turmeric, curry leaves and hing. ♦ Add puffed rice and mix well. ♦ Garnish with chopped coriander.
1 onion, diced (optional) 1/2 c potato, cut small (optional)	♦ Add chopped onions and/or potatoes as an option after the dals have been browned, and saute.

Rice Flour Upuma with Tamarind

Ingredients	Method
1 1/2 tsp tamarind paste 1/4 c hot water	Dissolve tamarind paste in hot water.
1 c rice flour 1 tsp salt	♦ In a bowl, mix rice flour, salt and tamarind water, and knead to a dough.
2-3 tbs oil 1 tsp mustard seeds	♦ Heat oil in a wok or deep frying pan. Add mustard seeds.
2 dry red chilies, cut small 1/8 tsp hing A pinch of turmeric	♦ As the seeds start to pop, add chilies; after a few seconds, add the rest of the ingredients and the dough. ♦ Fry the dough over low heat until it turns brown and does not stick to the fingers. Stir frequently.
3-4 curry leaves	♦ Add curry leaves and serve.

Note: This takes more oil than other varieties of upuma, as the rice flour needs to be well roasted. The tangy taste of tamarind gives it an interesting flavour.
Serve as a tea time snack along with a sweet dish.

Rava (Semolina) Upuma

1 c rava (semolina)	In a heated skillet, dry-roast rava and set aside.
2 tbs ghee 2 tbs oil 1 tsp mustard seeds	♦ In the same skillet, heat ghee and oil, and pop mustard seeds.
1 tbs channa dal 1 tbs urad dal 2 small green chilies, finely chopped 2 small red chilies, finely chopped 1 rounded tsp freshly grated ginger 1 tsp curry leaves	♦ Add dals, green chilies, ginger and curry leaves, and saute until browned.
1 medium sized onion, finely chopped	♦ Add onion and saute until translucent.

Rava Upuma - contd.

2 c water
1 1/2 tsp salt
1/4 tsp hing

- Add water, salt and hing, and continue to cook.

- As the water begins to boil, add the browned rava. Reduce heat and simmer while stirring to prevent lumps.

- Once the water is absorbed and the rava is fully cooked, remove from heat.

Ideal for a Sunday morning breakfast or as a light dinner, when combined with eggplant gotsu .

Note Finely chopped carrots, green beans, bell pepper and green peas (either all or in any combination, depending on availability) can be added after lightly sauteeing the onions. Adds colour and nutritional value. Make sure that you increase the quantity of water proportionately.

Rice Upuma

Ingredients	Method
3 tbs oil 1 1/2 tsp mustard seeds	In a heavy bottomed pan, heat oil and pop mustard seeds.
2 tbs urad dal 1 tbs channa dal 2 small dry red chilies, broken into pieces	♦ Add dals and chilies.
2 c water 1 1/2 tsp salt 1/2 tsp hing a few curry leaves 1/4 c grated, unsweetened coconut	♦ Saute until the dals are golden brown and add water. Add salt, hing and curry leaves, and finally, coconut (Add the coconut slowly to prevent boiling over). Bring to a boil over low to medium heat.
1 c cream of rice or Grits 1 tbs ghee	♦ Add cream of rice and stir until the water is mostly absorbed and the grains get half-cooked. ♦ Reduce heat and keep the pan covered. Simmer and stir occasionally until the rice gets cooked and the water gets absorbed completely. Add ghee for flavour.
Comment: This is the South Indian version of Polenta. Goes well with mint or coriander chutney or mango pickles.	

Onion Pakoda

Ingredients	Method
3 tsp melted ghee A pinch of baking soda	In a shallow bowl, mix ghee and baking soda together. Beat with a fork until the mixture foams.
1/2 c chickpea flour 1/4 c rice flour 1 tsp salt 1 tsp chili powder 1/4 tsp turmeric 3-4 curry leaves 1/2 c onion, diced 2 small green chilies, diced 1 tsp ginger, minced	♦ Add ingredients listed alongside to the contents of the bowl and knead. ♦ Do not add any water initially- the moisture of the onions is sufficient. ♦ After 5 minutes, add a few tbs water gradually and knead to a stiff dough.
Oil for frying	♦ Heat oil in a deep frying pan or wok over medium heat. ♦ Take a bit of the dough; break it into bite-sized dumplings and drop into the hot oil. Pakodas are left with jagged ends, not patted and smoothed into shape. Remove when golden brown. ♦ Serve with mint or coriander chutney. ♦ Best when eaten hot off the pan.

Adai

(Pancake-like preparation made from rice and lentils)

Ingredients	Method
1 c rice 1/2 c toor dal 1/2 c channa dal 1/4 c urad dal	**To prepare the dough:** In two separate bowls, soak rice and dals for about 2 hours.
1 1/2 tsp salt 3 small red chilies 3 small green chilies 1 tsp freshly grated ginger 4-6 tbs water A few curry leaves 2 tbs coriander 1/2 tsp hing	♦ Rinse rice and dals thoroughly; drain and grind coarsely in a blender along with salt, chilies and ginger. ♦ Grind in short spurts to a coarse paste, slowly adding water in small quantities. ♦ Add curry and coriander leaves, and grind for 5 more seconds. ♦ Transfer from blender into a bowl. Add hing and mix well with a spatula. ♦ The final consistency will be heavy and thick, neither dry nor runny.
Optional: 1 c onion, finely chopped and/ or 1 - 2 tbs coconut	♦ A tasty option is to add onions and/or shredded coconut to the batter.

A d a i - contd.

Oil for frying

Serve with a hot *chutney*, *Vattal Kuzhambu* or *sambar*. Some like it with butter or ghee and jaggery. One would normally try each *Adai* with a different accompaniment, discuss their relative merits and, of course, assert the superiority of one's own favourite!

To make the Adai:

- Heat skillet to a medium temperature as you would for pancakes.
- Spread a little batter with a spoon or by hand.
- Using a spatula, make 3 - 4 perforations in the middle of the batter and sprinkle about 1tbs oil over and around the *adai*. The thickness should be about 1/4".
- Once the bottom is golden brown, turn it over and sprinkle a little more oil. Remove and serve when both sides are a golden brown.

Comment: Two or three *Adais* - depending on individual capacity - along with the accompaniments, followed by yoghurt in some form make a complete meal.
This is one of those home-made preparations that one rarely comes across in restaurants even in India.

Dal Vadai

Ingredients	Method
1/2 c channa dal 1/2 c toor dal 1/8 cup urad dal 2 tbs moong dal	Soak dals in separate bowls for about 2 hours. ♦ Strain and rinse thoroughly. Drain.
1 1/2 tsp salt 2 small green chilies, finely chopped 3 small red chilies, finely chopped 1 tsp freshly grated ginger	♦ In a blender or food processor, mix the dals, salt, chilies, and ginger. Grind to a coarse paste without adding any water.
A few curry leaves 2 tbs chopped coriander 2 tbs cashews, quartered 1 tsp hing A pinch of baking soda 1 tsp ghee 1 c chopped onion (optional)	♦ Transfer to a mixing bowl and add the ingredients listed alongside. Mix well with a spatula.

Dal Vadai - contd.

Oil for frying	♦ Heat oil in a skillet. ♦ While the oil is heating, break up the dough into balls about the size of a golf ball. ♦ To get each dough-ball ready for frying: oil your left palm, flatten a ball on it to roughly 2" in diameter, tilt it on to the forefingers of your right hand and lower gently and quickly into the hot oil. ♦ Lower about 3-4 vadais at a time into hot oil in a skillet (rather like preparing *falafel*, if you are familiar with them). ♦ Fry both sides until golden brown. (You might want to practise with just one to test the oil temperature.) **Note:** This snack goes best with chutney or *sambar*. Optional: Add 1/2 c finely chopped onion to the dough after grinding.

Urad Dal Vadai

Ingredients	Method
1 c urad dal 1/4 c channa or toor dal	**To make the dough:** Soak dals for about 1 1/2 hours. ♦ Rinse thoroughly; drain.
1 tsp salt 3 small red chilies, finely chopped	♦ In a blender or food processor, place dals, salt and red chilies. Grind the mix for about 5 seconds without adding any water.
About 1/4 c water	♦ Alternately add water by the spoonful and pulse grind to a smooth, thick paste.
2 small green chilies, finely chopped 1 tsp freshly grated ginger 3 curry leaves or 1-2 tbs coriander, chopped 1/4 tsp hing	♦ Transfer paste to a mixing bowl; add ginger, green chilies, hing and curry leaves or coriander. Mix well with a spatula.
1 rounded tsp rice flour	♦ Add rice flour to the dough and mix thoroughly .

Urad Dal Vadai - contd.

Oil for frying

Comment: A very versatile snack, almost a must on festive occasions as one of the many supplements; makes an excellent duo with *idlis* as a wholesome breakfast or lunch.

To make the Vadais:

- Heat oil in a deep skillet or wok. Meanwhile, break the dough up into balls about 1 1/2 " in diameter.

  (For details on how to shape the *Vadais* before frying, see Note below.)

- When the oil is hot, gently slip about 3-4 *vadais* into the skillet, one at a time. Fry both sides until golden brown. You might want to practise with just one to test the oil temperature. This goes best with *chutney* or *sambar*.

Note: The *Vadai* is shaped like a doughnut (or the other way around, whichever you are more familiar with!) Take a small plastic sheet, smear with a few drops of oil and water, so that the dough does not stick to it. Keep a bowl of water nearby. Dip your fingers in the water, take out a ball of dough, flatten it gently on the sheet into a circular shape, 1/2" thick and 2" in diameter. Poke a hole in the middle. It should be thinner than a doughnut, as it puffs up while frying. Wetting the fingers again, tilt the *vadai* on to your right forefingers and slip it into hot oil. You can fry up to 4 *vadais* in one batch in a medium-sized wok.

Sevai

(Flavoured rice noodles)

In traditional South Indian homes, *sevai*-making days are major culinary events. Essentially a group activity, it would press every member of the family and friendly neighbours into service. The term 'service' is apt in more ways than one: the chef of the day would rightfully claim that she has done "great service," playing on the word '*sevai*' which means service.

The real *sevai* is a labour of love. The dough itself is a test of skill - rice flour, mixed with the right amount of water and kneaded to the right degree of softness, and then steamed for the right length of time to produce the right texture with no trace of lumps. And finally, the moment of magic, when balls of smooth, white dough disappear into the "sevai nazhi" (almost a reliquary, a contraption that calls for considerable physical strength), only to reappear as wriggly noodles.

The prelude to this drama started earlier with the preparation of a variety of differently flavoured mixtures. They are now waiting in the wings to mingle with portions of the *sevai* and to infuse colours and flavours into it...

The rice sticks available in supermarkets (I have used the "Dragon" brand from India and some varieties imported from Malaysia to great effect) do provide the taste experience of these dishes, if not the drama. Each brand has a different time-frame for cooking. Follow the package directions. The following pages give the recipes for the different flavourings.

Two or three varieties of *sevai* made from 100 gms of rice sticks should serve four to five hearty appetites.

Lemon Sevai

Ingredients	Method
2 c rice sticks broken into 1-1 1/2" bits 1/2 tsp salt	Cook broken rice sticks, following package directions and adding salt to the water while cooking. Drain completely.
4-5 tbs lemon juice 1 tsp salt 1/8 tsp turmeric 1/4 tsp hing	♦ Prepare lemon juice in a bowl. Combine with rest of the ingredients listed alongside.
2 tbs oil 1 1/2 tsp mustard seeds 2 or 3 green chilies, chopped	♦ Heat oil in skillet over medium heat. Add mustard seeds and chilies. When the seeds start to pop and the chilies begin to turn colour, add to the lemon juice. Stir well.
	♦ Mix three-fourths of the juice-mixture with the rice sticks. Add the rest according to taste. Left over juice can be stored in the refrigerator and used later in rasam or soup.
A few sprigs of coriander leaves, chopped	♦ Garnish with coriander.

Urad Dal Sevai

Ingredients	Method
2 c rice sticks (broken into 1- 1 1/2" bits) 1/2 tsp salt	Cook broken rice sticks, following package directions and adding salt to the water. Drain completely.
1 c urad dal 1 1/4 tsp salt 2-3 dry, red chilies	♦ Wash and soak urad dal for 2 hours. Wash again and drain. ♦ In a blender, grind the dal along with salt and red chilesi to a stiff dough, adding water little by little. ♦ Spread the dough about 1/2" thick in a greased container such as a double boiler and steam for 5-8 minutes. The dough will expand when cooked. Check that it is fully cooked by inserting a knife into the dough and making sure that it does not stick to the sides. ♦ Allow the dough to cool for 10 minutes and break it down by hand to a coarse texture, allowing no lumps to remain.
3-4 tbs oil 2 tsp mustard seeds	♦ Heat oil in a wok or shallow pan and pop mustard seeds.

Urad Dal Sevai - contd.

Ingredients	Method
1-2 small chopped green chilies A few curry leaves	♦ Add green chili, curry leaves and the dough, and saute over low heat for 8 - 10 minutes. Add more oil if the mix begins to stick to the pan.
1/4 cup shredded coconut	♦ Add coconut and keep stirring. The aroma comes through when well-blended and fried.
1/4 tsp hing	♦ Add hing and stir; remove from heat after a few seconds.
	♦ Mix in the cooked rice sticks.

Note: This can be served either hot or at room temperature.
Serve with *Mor Kuzhambu* and Mustard Seeds in Oil (see box at left; sprinkle a few spoons of this on the sevai according to taste).

Mustard Seeds in Oil:
In a small skillet, heat 5 tbs oil (preferably sesame oil) and add 5 to 6 tsp mustard seeds. As soon as seeds start to pop, remove from heat, pour into a metal bowl or container and add 1/4 tsp hing.

Coconut Sevai

Ingredients	Method
2 c rice sticks, broken into 1 - 1 1/2" bits 1/4 tsp salt	Cook broken rice sticks, following package directions and adding salt to the water. Drain completely.
2 tbs oil 2 tsp mustard seeds 2 tbs urad dal 2 green chilies, chopped 1dry, red chili, chopped	♦ Heat oil in a skillet over medium heat. Pop mustard seeds. ♦ Add urad dal and chilies.
1/2 c shredded coconut (preferably fresh) A few curry leaves 1 tsp salt	♦ As the dals get browned, add shredded coconut, curry leaves and salt. ♦ Keep stirring for about 3 minutes until you smell the aroma of fried coconut.
1/4 tsp hing	♦ Add hing, stir for a few seconds and remove from heat. ♦ Mix with cooked rice sticks. ♦ Serve with *mor kuzhambu* and/ or mint chutney.

Note: The ratio of coconut mix to rice sticks is a matter of individual preference. It is advisable not to mix the entire lot together in one go. Any left over coconut mix can be stored up to a week.

Yoghurt Sevai

Ingredients	Method
1 c rice sticks 1/4 tsp salt	Cook rice sticks. See instructions for previous recipe.
1 c plain, thick yoghurt 1/2 tsp salt A few sprigs of coriander, chopped	♦ Mix yoghurt, salt and coriander in a bowl. Stir lightly.
2 tsp oil 2 tsp mustard seeds 1 green chili, chopped	♦ In a mini wok or small skillet, heat oil. ♦ Add mustard seeds and chilies over medium heat. As soon as the seeds pop and the chilies get fried, add to the yoghurt. ♦ Mix the cooked rice sticks and blend well. The quantity of yoghurt may be varied according to taste.

Note: This is a quick recipe to use up left over *Sevai*.
General hint: Prepare the different seasonings at your convenience, even a day earlier. All you have to do on the day of the party is to cook the rice sticks and the accompaniment.

Sweet Sevai

Ingredients	Method
1 c rice sticks	Cook rice sticks. See instructions for lemon recipe. Do not add salt.
3/4 c jaggery or brown sugar	♦ If using Indian jaggery, make a thick syrup by heating 3/4 c powdered jaggery with just enough water to prevent burning. As soon as the powder melts, strain through a tea strainer.
1/2 c shredded coconut	♦ Pour into a cooking pan. After 2-3 minutes of heating, add shredded coconut. ♦ Keep stirring until the mixture thickens to a semi-solid state.
1/2 tsp cardamom powder	♦ Add cardamom and cooked rice sticks (*sevai*) and blend together.
2 tsp ghee 1 tbs cashews, broken into halves	♦ Brown cashews in heated ghee and add to the *sevai*.
	♦ Serve as the *grande finale* to a feast of *sevais* or by itself as a dessert in another meal.

Vegetable Gravies

The recipes in this section are the mainstay of a meal, complemented by a dry vegetable, *chutney*, *raita* or a salad. They are normally eaten either with rice - flavoured or plain - or with any of the Indian breads. A few north Indian recipes have been included at the end of this chapter, which go particularly well with chappatis or parathas, the staple flat bread of North Indian cuisine. These have become rather popular in cosmopolitan South Indian homes.

Like an Indian Raga or melody which unfolds freely within a given frame, the same dish can have more than one interpretation . This is particularly noticeable in the case of vegetable gravies. There will be subtle variation in taste, flavour and consistency from family to family and community to community.

As the final consistency is a delicate balance between so many variables, you may like to vary the amount of water specified depending on your individual preference.

These recipes are sure to explode the myth that Madras is synonymous with being chili-hot. Even so, exercise caution when you prepare a dish for the first time.

"Fortune will smile on the host who plays host with a smile".

- Tirukkural, chapter on Hospitality -

Vegetable Gravies

Sambar

(Bell pepper in tamarind-lentils sauce)

Ingredients	Method
1/2 c toor dal A pinch of turmeric	Cook toor dal - adding a pinch of turmeric - until soft (see Notes on page 10). Mash with a spoon when still warm.
1 small lemon-sized tamarind or 11/2 tsp of tamarind paste	♦ Extract 2 cups of juice from pulp (see Notes on page 12). Alternatively, dissolve tamarind paste in 2 c warm water.
1 onion, cut into small pieces or 10 to 12 pearl onions or shallots (peeled and whole) 1 bell pepper (small)	♦ Cut onion and bell pepper into big chunks. If using pearl onions or shallots, just peel them.
2 tbs oil 2 tsp melted butter 1 tsp mustard seeds 1/8 tsp fenugreek	♦ In a wok or a thick-bottomed cooking pan, heat oil and melted butter over medium heat; add mustard seeds and fenugreek. ♦ When seeds begin to crackle, add the cut onion pieces and bell pepper.

Sambar - contd.

Ingredients	Method
1 1/2 tsp salt 1 tsp sugar 1 1/2 tsp sambar powder (contains red chili)	♦ Saute onion and bell pepper for 5 minutes, allowing the onion to become translucent. Pour in the extracted tamarind water and add salt, sugar and sambar powder.
	♦ Boil for about 7 minutes on medium heat, by which time the vegetables should have been cooked and the spices well-blended. A third of the water should have evaporated.
	♦ Add the finely cooked dal. Boil again for 2 minutes, adding a little warm or hot water, if necessary, to arrive at the desired consistency.
1/4 tsp hing A few sprigs of coriander	♦ Add hing just before switching off the heat. Garnish with coriander and serve.

Note: Different varieties of sambar powder are now available in Indian grocery stores. For home-made recipe, see page 156. Other vegetables that could be used are okra or 'seng' (a foot-long hard-shelled thin gourd), if available.

Onion Sambar

(with ground masala)

Ingredients	Method
1 small lemon sized tamarind or 11/2 tsp tamarind paste	Prepare 2 c tamarind juice (see Notes on page 12). Set aside.
10 pearl onions or shallots (or 1 large red or yellow onion) 1 bell pepper	♦ Cut onion and bell pepper into big chunks. If using shallots or pearl onions, peel and leave whole.
1/2 c toor dal A pinch of turmeric	♦ Cook toor dal, adding turmeric (see Notes on page 10), to a soft consistency. Mash with a ladle.
3 tsp coriander seeds 2 tsp chana dal 1/2 tsp urad dal 3 small red chilies 1/8 tsp black pepper powder or 5-6 pepper corns 2 tbs shredded coconut	♦ In a warm skillet, using a tsp melted butter, saute all the ingredients listed alongside except the shredded coconut until the dals turn golden brown. Finally add the coconut and saute for another minute. Do not over-fry. ♦ Grind the fried ingredients to a smooth paste with very little water and set aside.
1 tbs melted butter 2 tsp oil 1 tsp mustard seeds	♦ In a thick-bottomed cooking pan, heat 2 tsp melted butter and 2 tsp oil over low heat. Add

Onion Sambar - contd.

1/8 tsp fenugreek	mustard seeds. When they begin to pop, add fenugreek. When they start to turn brown, add onion and bell pepper; saute until the onion turns translucent.
1 1/2 tsp salt	♦ Add tamarind water and salt and boil on medium heat for about 7 - 8 minutes until 1/3 of the water evaporates and the raw smell disappears.
	♦ Add the ground paste to the boiling tamarind water and stir well. Simmer for 5 minutes. By now, the ground masala should have blended well with the tamarind water.
1/4 tsp hing	♦ Add cooked toor dal and 1/2 - 1 c hot water, depending on desired consistency. Bring to a boil; add hing and allow to simmer for 5 minutes.
A few sprigs of coriander leaves	♦ Add chopped coriander and mix. Serve.

Note The flavour of very small shallot like onions is what one would associate with this dish; substitutes are second best. Goes well with rice, *idli*, *dosai* and *vadai*. Adding cashew nuts (2 tbs) fried in melted butter enhances the taste (as a final garnish).

Potato Rasavangi

(Sweet and sour variation of Sambar)

Ingredients	Method
1 tbs oil	Heat oil.
1 tbs coriander seeds 1 tbs channa dal 1 tsp urad dal 3 small red chilies 4 tbs shredded coconut	♦ On low to medium heat, fry the first four ingredients listed alongside until the dals turn golden brown. Add shredded coconut at the very end, and grind the mixture in a blender to a coarse paste with very little water. Set aside.
3 medium potatoes (about 2 1/2 c, cut up)	♦ Boil the potatoes, peel and cut into big chunks. As they will be boiled again, avoid over-cooking.
1/2 c toordal	♦ Cook toordal. (see Notes on page 10). Mash with a ladle when still warm.
Tamarind (half a lemon size) or 1 1/2 tsp of paste	♦ Prepare 2 c tamarind water in a saucepan. (see Notes on page 12)
1 tsp salt 1/4 tsp turmeric	♦ Add salt and turmeric, and bring to a boil over medium heat.

Rasavangi - contd.

Ingredients	Method
	♦ After 3 minutes, add the potatoes and cook for another 3 minutes.
2 tbs sugar	♦ When the potatoes are soft and well blended with tamarind and salt, add the ground paste and boil for 5 more minutes. Add cooked toordal and sugar. You may need to add 1/2 - 1 c hot water at this stage, depending on desired consistency.
	♦ Bring to a boil and simmer for 5 minutes before removing.
1 tbs oil 1 tsp mustard seeds 1/2 tsp urad dal 1/4 tsp hing	♦ Heat oil in a small wok or skillet and add mustard seeds. As they start to crackle, add urad dal and hing, and brown. Add to the gravy.
A few sprigs of coriander	♦ Add coriander and serve with rice.

Comment Eggplant can be substituted for potatoes (they do not have to be pre-boiled). For best results, use Japanese or Indian varieties of eggplant, unpeeled and cut in chunks. Soak eggplant chunks in water for 10 minutes to remove the acidity. Brown sugar or jaggery is preferable to white sugar.

Paruppu

(Lentils with tomatoes)

Ingredients	Method
1/2 c toordal 1/2 c moong dal	Cook the two dals together, preferably in a pressure cooker (see Notes on page 10). ♦ Mash with a spoon.
1 tbs ghee 1 tbs oil 1 tsp mustard seeds 1/2 tsp cumin seeds 1 small onion (finely chopped) 2 or 3 small green chilies (finely chopped)	♦ In a skillet, heat ghee and oil together. On medium heat, add mustard seeds. Once they begin to crackle, add cumin, onions and chilies, and saute until onions are translucent. ♦ In a cooking pan, combine the sauteed mixture and the cooked dal.
1/2 tsp salt 1/4 tsp turmeric A pinch of hing	♦ Add salt, turmeric and hing. Add 1/2 c water (more if you would like a runny consistency) and cook on low to medium heat until it starts to bubble up.
2 small tomatoes, chopped Juice of 1/2 lemon A few sprigs of coriander	♦ Remove from heat; add lemon juice, coriander and chopped tomatoes while the dal is still hot. Serve with *chappatis* or *parathas*.

Comment: A variation would be to saute the tomatoes before adding to the cooked dal.

Spinach Koottu

(Spinach with coconut)

Ingredients	Method
3 c fresh chopped spinach (or one 8 or 10oz packet, frozen)	Cook spinach, covered, with no additional water.
2 tbs oil	♦ Heat oil.
2 tsp urad dal 1 tsp cumin seeds 6 black pepper corns 1 small red chili	♦ Fry the ingredients listed alongside on medium heat until the dal turns golden brown .
1/2 c shredded coconut	♦ Grind this along with the coconut to a coarse paste with very little water. Set aside.
1 tsp salt 1 - 1 1/2 c water	♦ In a saucepan, place cooked spinach and ground masala. Add salt and water, and boil for 3 minutes over medium heat.
1 tbs melted butter 1 tsp mustard seeds	♦ Season with mustard seeds popped in butter (see Notes on page 11).

Comment: This makes a nice side dish with *sambar* and rice and goes equally well with *chappatis*. For additional flavour add 1/4 cup coconut milk.

Spinach with Onions and lentils

Ingredients	Method
1/2 c toor dal	Cook toor dal (see Notes on page 10).
3 c fresh spinach (or one 8 or 10 oz. packet frozen)	♦ Wash, chop and cook spinach with no additional water on low heat.
Tamarind (half a lemon size) or 1 tsp tamarind paste 1 tsp salt 1 tsp sambar powder	♦ Prepare 1 1/2 c tamarind water (see Notes on page 12). Mix tamarind water with cooked spinach and add salt and sambar powder. Cook for 5-7 minutes on medium heat until the raw smell of the tamarind disappears. ♦ Add cooked toor dal and 1/2 - 1 c hot water. Cook for another 5 minutes on low to medium heat.
2 tbs ghee or oil 1/2 tsp mustard seeds 1 c onion, finely chopped	♦ To ghee or oil in a skillet, add mustard seeds. As they begin to crackle, add chopped onion and saute on low to medium heat. ♦ Once the onion becomes translucent, add to the spinach-lentil mix and serve.

Comment
Goes with rice as well as *chappatis*.

Spinach with spiced lentils and potatoes

Ingredients	Method
1/2 c channa dal	Soak channa dal in water for 10 minutes; drain.
Tamarind (1/2 lemon size), soaked in 1 cup water or 1 tsp paste	♦ Extract 1c concentrated tamarind juice (see Notes on page 12).
2 c fresh cut spinach (or one 8 oz. packet frozen) 1 c diced onion 4 cloves of garlic, chopped 1/2 c potatoes, cubed 1 c tomato, cubed 2 small green chilies 1/4 tsp turmeric 1 1/2 tsp salt	♦ Combine ingredients listed alongside with the channa dal; cook in covered saucepan with just enough water to cover the vegetables. ♦ Remove when cool and mash coarsely either with a ladle or a hand mixer . ♦ Add the strained tamarind water to the mixture and boil uncovered for 5 minutes.
1 tsp ghee 1/4 tsp mustard seeds A pinch of hing 3/4 tsp cumin powder	♦ In a small skillet or wok, heat ghee. ♦ Add mustard seeds, hing and cumin powder. Saute until seeds pop and add to the spinach mix.

Spinach with spiced lentils - contd.

Optional ingredients: 1/4 c fenugreek leaves **or** 1/2 tsp fenugreek powder A few sprigs of coriander	♦ Either or both optional ingredients may be added and blended just before serving. A great accompaniment to rice as well as *chappatis*.

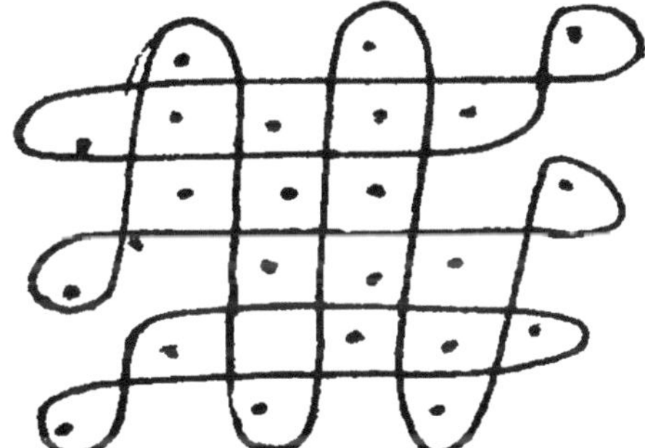

Aviyal

(Vegetable stew with yoghurt)

Ingredients	Method
1/2 c green beans, chopped 1/4 c green peas 1/4 c lima beans 1/2 c carrot, cubed 1/2 c potato, cubed 1/2 chayote squash, cubed 1/2 c zucchini, chopped 1 1/2 tsp salt 1/4 tsp turmeric powder	Wash and place vegetables in a saucepan, adding sal, turmeric and just enough water to cover. ♦ Let the vegetables get half-cooked over medium heat.
1/2 c shredded coconut, (unsweetened) 3 small green chilies 1tsp cumin seeds 3 tsp rice	♦ Grind the ingredients listed alongside to a smooth paste with very little water. ♦ Add to the half-cooked vegetables. Cook until well-blended about 3-4 minutes over medium heat.
8 oz. carton yoghurt 1 tsp gravy flour	♦ Add gravy flour to the yoghurt. Stir well and add to the vegetables. Reduce heat and

allow the yoghurt to blend well with the vegetables. Do not let it boil.

Ingredients	Method
2 tbs oil (preferably coconut oil) 1/2 tsp mustard seeds A sprig of curry leaves	♦ Heat oil; add mustard seeds and curry leaves. As the seeds start to crackle, remove from heat and add to the gravy.

Comment Goes well with plain rice, *chappati* or *venpongal*. Chayote and zucchini make very good substitutes for white pumpkin, normally used in this recipe in India. Using fresh coconut gives a better flavour than the shredded coconut from supermarkets. If good quality canned coconut milk is available, 1/4 cup of it can be added while grinding the ingredients. It is advisable to keep the yoghurt at room temperature overnight, as the recipe calls for sour yoghurt.

Suggested composition

Plain white rice or *Venpongal*
Aviyal
Crunchy Potatoes
Fried papads

Mor Kuzhambu

(Buttermilk Gravy)

Ingredients	Method
6 or 7 tender okra	Wash and dry okra; cut into 1" pieces.
2 tbs oil	♦ In a skillet, brown the okra in oil and set aside.
4 tbs shredded coconut 2 small green chilies 3 tsp coriander seeds 1tsp grated ginger 1 tsp cumin seeds	♦ Grind the ingredients listed alongside to a smooth paste, adding very little water.
1 1/2 c thick yoghurt, blended with 1/2 c water **or** 2 c buttermilk 1 tsp salt 1tsp gravy flour	♦ Add the ground paste, salt and gravy flour to yoghurt or buttermilk and stir well. (As an alternative to gravy flour, you can add 1 tbs raw rice to the ingredients to be ground) ♦ Bring to a boil on low heat and remove at once, as it tends to boil over.

Mor Kuzhambu - contd.

Ingredients	Method
1 tbs oil 1 tsp mustard seeds 1/8 tsp fenugreek seeds	♦ Add the browned okra. Season with mustard and fenugreek in oil. (see Notes on page 11)
A sprig of curry leaves	♦ Add curry leaves and serve.

Suggested composition:
Plain rice
Mor kuzhambu
Paruppu usili
Salad with grated carrots

Comment: You should be able to buy ready buttermilk. To make it a little sour, keep it at room temperature overnight. As an alternative to buttermilk, stir yoghurt with an eggbeater, adding a little water to make it thinner. Leave it unrefrigerated overnight to make it sour.

Poritha Kuzhambu

(Mixed vegetables in a lentils and coconut gravy)

1/2 c toordal	Wash, cook toordal (see Notes on page 10) and set aside.
1/2 c potato, cubed 1/2 c fresh green beans, chopped 1/4 c green peas 1/4 c lima beans or mixed vegetables	♦ Wash and cut vegetables and place in a cooking pan. Add just enough water to cover.
1 1/2 tsp salt 1 tsp sambar powder 1/4 tsp turmeric	♦ Add salt, sambar powder and turmeric, and bring to a boil. Simmer until vegetables are half-cooked.
1 tsp oil 2 tsp urad dal 1 tsp cumin seeds 4-5 black pepper corns 4 tbs shredded coconut	♦ Meanwhile, fry urad dal, black pepper and cumin in a skillet in oil until the dal turns golden brown. Finally add the shredded coconut. Remove from heat. ♦ Grind coarsely in a blender with very little water. ♦ Combine with vegetables and cooked toordal and bring to a boil.

Poritha Kuzhambu - contd.

A few curry leaves 1/4 tsp hing	♦ Add curry leaves and hing. Simmer for a minute.
1 tbs oil 1 tsp mustard seeds 1 tsp urad dal	♦ Season with mustard seeds and urad dal fried in oil (see Notes on page 11).

Suggested composition:
Rice
Poritha Kuzhambu
Okra fry
Raita of choice

Comment:
The consistency should be neither too thick nor too runny. Adding two tbs coconut milk (either fresh or canned) in the final stage enhances the flavour.

Poritha Koottu

(Mixed vegetables in a coconut gravy)

Ingredients	Method
1 c green beans 1/2 c green peas 1/2 c lima beans 1 c diced carrots 1/2 c potato, cubed	Wash and cut vegetables and place them in a cooking pan with just enough water to cover.
1 tsp salt 1/2 tsp turmeric 1/2 tsp sambar powder	♦ Add salt, turmeric and sambar powder, and cook on medium heat until vegetables are half-cooked.
1/2 c shredded coconut 2 tsp cumin seed 2 small red chilies	♦ In a blender, grind ingredients listed alongside to a smooth paste, adding a little water. ♦ Add to the vegetables and cook about 3 - 5 minutes longer. ♦ Add enough water for desired consistency. If it is too thin, add some gravy flour.
1 tsp hing A sprig of curry leaves	♦ Add hing and curry leaves. Simmer for a minute.

Poritha Koottu - contd.

1 tbs oil 1 tsp mustard seeds 1 tsp urad dal	♦ Season with mustard seeds and urad dal (see Notes on page 11). ♦ Serve with rice or *chappati*.

Cabbage Koottu

(Cabbage in a lentils & coconut gravy)

Ingredients	Method
1/4 c moong dal	Wash and cook moong dal; set aside (see Notes on page 10).
1/2 c finely chopped cabbage 1 c carrots, cut small 1 c potato, cut small 1/2 c green peas	♦ Place the washed and cut vegetables in a saucepan and add enough water to cover.
1 tsp salt 1 tsp sambar powder A pinch of turmeric	♦ Add salt, sambar powder and turmeric, and cook over medium heat until vegetables are half-cooked.
2 small green chilies 1 tsp cumin seeds 4 tbs shredded coconut	♦ Meanwhile, grind the ingredients listed alongside to a smooth paste, adding a little water. ♦ Add to vegetables and bring to a boil.

Cabbage Koottu - contd.

	♦ Add the cooked dal, stir and simmer for 5 minutes until well-blended.
4 curry leaves 1/4 tsp hing	♦ Add hing and curry leaves, and simmer for a minute.
1 tbs oil or melted butter 1 tsp mustard seeds 1 tsp urad dal	♦ Season with mustard seeds and urad dal fried in oil (see Notes on page 11). ♦ Goes well with *chappatis* or rice.

Eggplant with tamarind

Ingredients	Method
1 large eggplant (1/2 lb. or 200 - 250 gms.)	Rub eggplant with oil. Bake it at 375º for about 30 minutes until the skin is almost charred. Under cool running water, remove the skin. Once cool, mash coarsely.
Tamarind (half a lemon size) or 1 tsp paste	♦ Extract 1/2 c light tamarind water (see Notes on page 12), and mix with mashed eggplant.
1 tsp salt 1/4 tsp turmeric 1/4 tsp hing	♦ Add salt, turmeric and hing, and boil for 3 minutes on medium heat.
1 tbs oil 1 tsp mustard seeds 2 small green chilies, chopped fine	♦ In a small skillet or wok, saute mustard seeds in oil. Once they begin to pop, add green chilies. ♦ After a few seconds, remove from heat and add to the eggplant.

Eggplant with Tamarind - contd.

1/2 tsp jaggery (or brown sugar) A few sprigs of coriander (cilantro), chopped	♦ Add jaggery and stir. Garnish with coriander and serve.

Yoghurt variation : Prepare the eggplant as described above. Mash with a ladle. Add salt. Mix in one carton (8 oz.) of yoghurt and 2 tbs sour cream and blend them together. Garnish with coriander. In a small pan, heat oil, add mustard seeds and a chopped green chili. As the seeds begin to crackle, add to prepared dish. Serve with hot *chappatis* or rice.

Comment: The final consistency is stew-like. If you have a gas cooking range or barbecue grill, you could more easily bake the eggplant in the grill. Char-broil eggplant with the skin to achieve right degree of softness inside.

Eggplant Gotsu

(stew-like)

Ingredients	Method
A small lemon sized chunk of tamarind or 1tsp of tamarind paste	Extract 1 1/2 c tamarind water (see Notes on page 12).
1/4 c moong dal	♦ Cook moong dal to a soft consistency and set aside.
1 1/2 c eggplant, cut small	♦ Cut eggplant into very small pieces (the long, green variety is preferable, if available).
2 tbs oil 1 tsp mustard seeds 2 small green chilies, chopped 1 tsp grated ginger 1 c onions, diced	♦ Heat oil in a saucepan; add mustard seeds, green chilies and ginger. ♦ When the seeds begin to pop, add the onions and saute for 3 minutes on slow to medium heat. ♦ Add the eggplant and saute 5 minutes longer.
1 tsp salt A pinch of turmeric	♦ Add tamarind water, salt and turmeric, and boil for 7-8 minutes over medium heat, until the raw smell of the tamarind disappears.

Gotsu (Stewlike) - contd.

Ingredients	Method
1/2 to 1 c hot water	♦ Add the cooked moong dal and hot water, and simmer for 3 minutes.
1 tsp brown sugar 1/8 tsp hing	♦ Add brown sugar and hing and simmer for a minute more.
A few sprigs of coriander	♦ Garnish with coriander and serve.

Note: Consistency should be that of a thick soup.
A great accompaniment to *chappatis*.
Also goes with rice

Eggplant Gotsu

(without onions)

Ingredients	Method
1 large eggplant (1/2 lb. or 200 - 250 gms)	Wash eggplant, cut off the stem and make a slit lengthwise. Bake at 375º until the eggplant is nearly charred, turning over frequently for even baking.
1 tsp salt	♦ Place the eggplant under cool water and remove the skin. Mash and add salt.
Tamarind (size of half a lemon) or 1/2 tsp tamarind paste	♦ Extract 2 c tamarind water (see Notes on page 12).
A pinch of turmeric	♦ Add turmeric to the tamarind water and allow to boil on medium heat. As it begins to boil, add the mashed eggplant and cook for 7-10 minutes on low to medium heat.

Gotsu (without onions) - contd.

Ingredients	Method
1 tsp brown sugar A pinch of hing	♦ Add brown sugar and hing. Simmer for a minute.
2 tbs oil 1/2 tsp mustard seeds 1 or 2 small red chilies, finely chopped	♦ In a skillet, saute mustard seeds and red chilies until the seeds have crackled; combine with eggplant.
A few sprigs of coriander (cilantro)	♦ Garnish with coriander and serve. ♦ Goes with any of the Indian "bread" varieties.

Note: The eggplant can also be roasted on a gas range. Smear the eggplant with a little oil and roast it on top of the range. Turn it over frequently until the skin gets charred all over.

Milagu Kuzhambu

(Black Pepper Sauce)

Ingredients	Method
1 tbs ghee 2 tbs coriander seeds 1 tbs toordal 1/2 tsp cumin 1/2 tsp black pepper corns 3 large, dry red chilies	Fry the ingredients listed alongside in ghee until the dals turn golden brown. Grind the ingredients dry at first. Add a little water and grind again to form a smooth paste.
2 c water 1 1/2 tsp tamarind paste 1 1/2 tsp salt 1 tsp turmeric 1 tsp brown sugar	♦ In a saucepan, combine the items listed alongside and boil for 5 minutes on medium heat, stirring once in a while. ♦ Add the ground paste and stir well to avoid lumps. Let it simmer on low heat for 10-15 minutes until thickened.
1/4 tsp hing 1 tbs oil 1 tsp mustard seeds 5-6 fenugreek seeds A sprig of curry leaves	♦ Add hing and simmer for a minute longer. Season with mustard and fenugreek seeds sauteed in oil (see Notes on page 11), and stir. Add curry leaves and serve.

Note: Goes very well with *Venpongal*, Rice *upuma* or plain rice. You could also add okra to the sauce. Cut the vegetables approximately 1" long, saute until browned, and add to the sauce at the end of step two.

Vattal Kuzhambu

(Condensed tamarind sauce with onions)

Ingredients	Method
A lemon-sized chunk of tamarind (or 2 tsp tamarind paste)	Prepare 2 c tamarind water (see Notes on page 12).
3 tbs oil 2 tsp mustard seeds 1 1/2 tsp toor dal 1/2 tsp fenugreek 2 tsp peanuts (optional) 8-10 pearl onions or shallots	♦ In a heavy-bottomed cooking pan, heat oil. On medium heat, pop mustard seeds. Add the other seasoning as well as the peeled shallots. Stir until golden brown.
1 1/2 tsp salt 2 1/2 tsp sambar powder 1 tsp brown sugar 1/4 tsp hing A few curry leaves	♦ Add tamarind water, salt and sambar powder. ♦ Boil for 10 minutes on low to medium heat until the quantity is reduced to about 1 1/2 cups. ♦ Add brown sugar and hing. Continue to boil for 2 more minutes. Add curry leaves and remove from heat.

Note: If the consistency is too thin, add 1 tsp gravy flour mixed with 2 tsp water to the sauce. Allow to come to a boil before removing from heat. Goes very well with *Adai* or *Ven pongal*.A combination of *Vattal kuzhambu* and plain rice, acompanied by *Paruppu Tuvaiyal* and roasted papads spells nostalgia for South Indians living away from home, and is highly recommended by the initiated as an antidote for frayed nerves!

Potatoes and PeasKoottu

(with powdered spices)

3 tbs oil 1 tsp mustard seeds 1 c onions, chopped 2 small green chilies, chopped 100 gms potatoes, cubed (about 1 c) 2 medium tomatoes, chopped	To heated oil in a skillet, add mustard seeds. Once they begin to pop, add onion, green chilies and potatoes. Stir on low to medium heat.
1 1/2 tsp coriander powder 1 tsp chili powder 1 tsp cumin powder A pinch of turmeric 1/4 tsp ground black pepper powder 1/2 tsp garlic powder 1 tsp salt	♦ After 3 minutes, add the items listed alongside and keep stirring until the vegetables are well coated with the spices.
1/2 c green peas	♦ Add peas; when they are about half cooked, add tomatoes and

Potatoes and Peas Koottu - contd.

	simmer until the tomato juice gets absorbed. (**Note:** If you would like the consistency to be less thick, add 1/2 c water or tomato juice at this point.)
A few sprigs of coriander (cilantro)	♦ Garnish with coriander and serve.

Comment This is a simple version of this recipe. The same vegetables are treated to additional flavours in the following, more elaborate recipe.

Potatoes and Peas Koottu

(with ground masala)

Ingredients	Method
1/4 lb. (100 gm.) potatoes (about 2 medium)	Boil potatoes, peel and cut into small pieces. Do not over-cook potatoes because they have to be cooked again.
1 c onion, chopped 2 cloves garlic 2 small green chilies 1 tsp grated ginger A few sprigs of coriander 3 cardamoms, peeled 2 tsp shredded coconut	♦ Grind ingredients listed alongside to a semi-smooth paste.
2 tbs oil 2 tbs ghee 1/2 tsp mustard seeds	♦ In a skillet, heat oil and ghee on low to medium heat; add mustard seeds.
1 c onion, finely chopped	♦ Once the seeds begin to crackle, add onions and saute.

Potatoes and Peas Koottu - contd.

Ingredients	Method
	♦ Add the ground masala and stir well until the water is absorbed and the oil floats. By now, the masala will be well-cooked and not stick to the pan. ♦ Add 1 1/2 c water and blend well with the masala.
1/4 tsp turmeric 1 tsp salt 1 c green peas	♦ Add turmeric, salt, peas and potatoes, and continue to cook over low heat for 10 minutes more until it thickens. Add 1/4 c more water and continue to cook until it thickens once again.
1 tsp sugar A few sprigs of coriander (cilantro)	♦ Add sugar and coriander. Stir and serve. ♦ Goes well with rice or *chappatis*.

Peas Koottu

Ingredients	Method
1 c onions, chopped small 2 cloves garlic 1/2 tsp cinnamon A marble-sized chunk of tamarind 2 medium tomatoes, chopped small 2 tbs grated coconut 3 small green chilies, chopped 1 tsp brown sugar 1 tsp coriander seeds	Grind all the ingredients listed alongside together in a processor to a smooth paste, adding very little water.
3 tbs oil 1 tsp mustard seeds A pinch of turmeric	♦ Pop mustard seeds in oil; add masala paste and turmeric. Keep stirring on low to medium heat.
1 c green peas	♦ Once the water is absorbed and the masala is browned, add peas and 1/2 c water. Cook for 7 minutes on low heat until thickened.
A few sprigs of coriander	♦ Garnish with coriander and serve with *chappatis*.

Vegetable Masala Koottu

Ingredients	Method
1 medium sized potato 1/2 c peas 1/2 c green beans, cut into small pieces 1 c cauliflower 1 c red onions	Wash and cut all vegetables to desired size.
1 1/2 tsp cumin seeds 1 1/2 tsp coriander seeds 1/2 tsp ground black pepper 1/2 tsp turmeric powder 4 tbs cashew nuts 1/2 tsp chili powder	♦ Grind ingredients listed alongside in a processor to a fine powder.
3 tbs oil 1 tsp mustard seeds 1 tsp salt	♦ Pop mustard seeds in oil on medium heat. Add onions and masala powder, and saute until onions are translucent. ♦ Add vegetables and salt. Stir once in a while until the mixture is almost cooked.
2 medium tomatoes, chopped 2 tbs chopped coriander	♦ Add tomatoes and coriander. Cook on low heat for another 5 minutes until everything is well blended.

A semi-liquid curry to go with *chappatis*.

Dum Alu

Ingredients	Method
1/2 lb. potatoes (about 2 c), cut into 1 1/2" chunks	Wash the potatoes. Deep fry in oil and set aside. Instead of deep frying, you may also saute the potatoes in 3 tbs oil until they are browned.
1/2 c onion, chopped 1 tbs coriander seeds 2 small red chilies 3 cardamom pods 1 tbs shredded coconut 1/4 tsp ground black pepper 3 or 4 garlic cloves 1/2 tsp poppy seeds	♦ Grind ingredients listed alongside to a smooth paste without adding any water.
3 to 4 tbs oil 1 tbs ghee 1 tsp mustard seeds 1/2 c onion (finely chopped)	♦ In a skillet, heat oil and ghee; pop mustard seeds on medium heat. ♦ Add onions and saute until translucent. ♦ Add ground masala and continue to cook in oil on low to medium

Dum Alu - contd.

Ingredients	Method
	heat until the oil separates and the masala is slightly browned. Transfer to a cooking pan.
1 c water 1 tsp salt 1/2 tsp turmeric 1 tbs sugar	♦ Add water, salt, turmeric, sugar and the sauteed potatoes. Simmer until the gravy thickens. Add 1/2 c more hot water and allow to simmer for 5 more minutes.
2 large tomatoes, chopped A sprig of coriander	♦ Adjust salt to taste. Add chopped tomatoes and coriander and serve.

Comment A slight variation would be to brown the chopped tomatoes before adding to the dish.
Makes an excellent combination with *chappatis* or *parathas*.

Vegetable Koruma

Ingredients	Method
1/2 c carrot, cubed 1/2 c potato, cubed 10 green beans, chopped 1/2 c green peas 1 c cauliflower	Cut, wash and steam all the vegetables and set aside. Do not overcook, as they have to be cooked again.
1 medium onion, chopped 3 small green chilies 1 tbs ground fresh ginger 4-5 sprigs coriander leaves 2 cloves garlic 1 tbs coriander seeds 2 tbs shredded coconut 1/2 tsp poppy seeds 3 pods cardamom 1/4 tsp cinnamon	♦ Grind the ingredients listed alongside into a smooth paste with very little water.
3 tbs oil 1 tbs ghee 1/2 tsp mustard seeds	♦ In a deep - preferably nonstick - saucepan, heat oil and ghee; add mustard seeds on medium heat. When they begin to pop, add

Vegetable Koruma - contd.

Ingredients	Method
1 medium onion, chopped 1/4 tsp allspice	chopped onions and allspice. Stir and fry for 3 minutes.
	♦ Add the ground masala and keep stirring until it does not stick to the finger and oil starts to float.
1 tsp salt	♦ Add 1/2 - 3/4 c water and salt, and simmer for 3 minutes.
	♦ Add the steamed vegetables and simmer for another 5 minutes. Serve with rice or *chappatis*.

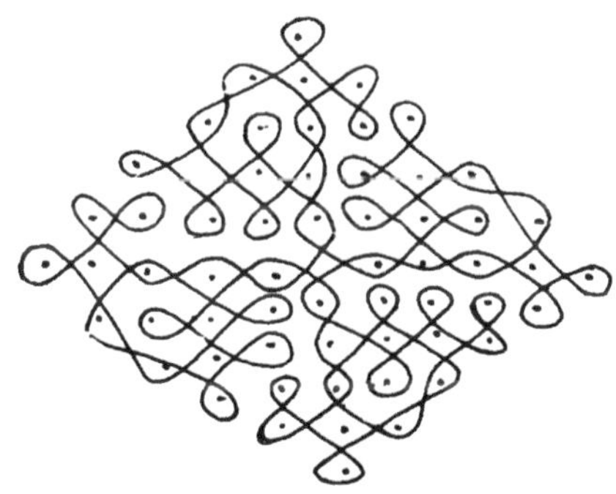

Paneer Kofta in Spinach Masala

(Soft cheese balls in a spicy spinach sauce)

Ingredients for Koftas

6 oz paneer (cottage cheese)
4 tbs plain flour
2 tbs chopped coriander
2 green chilies, chopped
A pinch of baking soda
Cooking oil

Method of making koftas

Drain cottage cheese thoroughly in a cheese cloth. Mix with all ingredients except oil and shape into small (1 1/2" diameter) balls.

- Heat oil and deep fry kofta balls to a golden brown. Drain on paper towels.

Ingredients for Spinach Masala

1 tbs fresh grated coconut
1 tbs chopped cashews
1tbs poppy seeds
3 cloves garlic, crushed
4-5 green chilies, chopped
1" piece of ginger, grated
1 tsp fennel seed (optional)

Method of making Spinach Masala

- In a blender or food processor, grind the ingredients listed alongside to a smooth paste.

Paneer Kofta in Spinach - contd.

Ingredients	Method
9 oz. finely chopped spinach	♦ Cook the spinach. When soft, put in a blender or processor and puree.
2tbs ghee	♦ Heat ghee and fry the ground ingredients on low to medium heat for 3-4 minutes.
1/2 c yoghurt	♦ Add yoghurt and continue cooking the masala over low heat for 2-3 minutes.
1/2 tsp sugar salt to taste	♦ Add spinach puree, sugar and salt, and cook for 2 more minutes. ♦ Just before serving, add the koftas to the spinach masala and heat thoroughly. ♦ Serve with mustard or sesame rice.

Note: The Indian variety of *paneer* is available in Indian grocery stores in the frozen food section.

Rajma

(Red kidney beans in tomato gravy)

Ingredients	Method
1 c cooked red kidney beans (8 oz. canned kidney beans)	If using canned kidney beans, wash and drain. If using fresh beans, soak 1/3 c overnight in water; rinse and cook until tender in 1 c water.
1tsp grated ginger 3 cloves garlic 3 tbs chopped coriander (cilantro) 1 tbs coriander seeds 3 pods cardamom	♦ Keeping aside a little coriander for garnish, grind ingredients listed alongside to a smooth paste with 1 - 2 tbs water.
3 tbs ghee 1 c red onions, finely chopped	♦ Heat ghee in a skillet and saute onion to a golden brown on medium heat. ♦ Add the ground paste and saute for 3 minutes on low to medium heat until browned.
1 c tomatoes, finely chopped	♦ Add tomatoes and cook covered for 3 minutes.

Rajma - contd.

Ingredients	Method
1 tsp turmeric 1 tsp chili powder 1 1/2 tsp salt 3/4 c water 1 tbs fresh cream 2 tbs ghee A few sprigs of coriander, chopped	♦ Add turmeric, chili powder, salt and beans. Add water and simmer until everything is well-blended and the gravy thickens. ♦ Add cream, ghee and coriander, and stir.
1 tsp sugar 1/2 tsp garam masala powder	♦ Add sugar and garam masala and mix thoroughly. ♦ Goes well with *chappatis* as well as rice.

Suggested composition

Rice or *chappati*
Rajma
Okra *raita*

Rasam

Rasam may be translated as essence or flavour. In its variety and refinement, it is unique to the South Indian cuisine.

It is normally eaten mixed with rice and comes in as a light interlude after the first round of vegetable gravy and rice, and before rounding up the meal with yoghurt. But it is becoming increasingly common to serve it first as an appetiser, especially at parties, when the menu is somewhat elaborate.

Connoisseurs of *rasam* vary distinctly in their preference. Some like it as a clear broth - *telivu rasam* - (in which case the sediment of lentils and seasoning will be 'recycled' later), and others like it "stirred". Incidentally, the practice in India would be to drink the *rasam* from a mug, but it can just as easily be served in a soup bowl.

There are two advantages to this: you get to consume a little less rice (better for the waistline or reserve capacity for other things, whichever way you want to look at it) and you get to enjoy the taste, flavour and aroma of the *rasam* for itself and by itself.

Rasam

"With a guest waiting at the door,
even immortalising nectar is unworthy of eating."
- Tirukkural , chapter on Hospitality -

Lemon Rasam

Ingredients	Method
1/2 c toordal	Cook toordal to a soft consistency. When cool, mash with a ladle.
1/2 c tomato juice 1 c water 1 tsp salt 1/4 tsp turmeric	♦ Add water, tomato juice, salt and turmeric, and bring to a boil.
2 tbs ghee 2 medium tomatoes, chopped	♦ Saute tomatoes in ghee and add to the liquid.
1/4 tsp hing	♦ Add hing. When the rasam starts to foam, remove from heat. (**Caution:** Rasam will lose all flavour, if boiled for too long).
1 tbs ghee 1/2 tsp mustard seeds 2 small green chilies, finely chopped	♦ In a skillet, heat ghee; add mustard seeds and green chilies. When the mustard seeds pop, add to the rasam.
2 tbs lemon juice A few sprigs of coriander	♦ Add lemon juic and stir well. Garnish with coriander and serve.

Tomato & Lentil Rasam

Ingredients	Method
Tamarind, marble-sized chunk or 1/4 tsp tamarind paste	Soak tamarind in warm water for 5-10 minutes and extract 1 1/2 c water; or dissolve tamarind paste in 1 1/2 c warm water (see Notes on page 12).
1/4 c toordal	♦ Cook toordal (see Notes on page 10). Once cool, mash with a ladle to a smooth consistency. Add 1 1/2 c water and stir. Set aside.
1 tsp salt 1 tsp rasam or sambar powder 1 tsp sugar	♦ Pour the extracted tamarind water into a saucepan; add salt, rasam (or sambar) powder and sugar. ♦ Bring to a boil and then simmer over low to medium heat for 10 minutes until about a quarter of the water evaporates and the raw smell of the rasam/sambar powder disappears.
2 tomatoes, chopped	♦ Add tomatoes (or 1/2 c tomato juice) and boil for 2 more minutes.

Tomato & Lentil Rasam - contd.

Ingredients	Method
1/4 tsp hing	♦ Add the toordal water and hing, and bring to a boil. ♦ When the liquid starts to foam, remove from heat.
1 tbs ghee 1/2 tsp mustard seeds 1/4 tsp ground black pepper 1/2 tsp cumin	♦ In a separate skillet or mini wok, heat ghee; add mustard seeds, ground pepper and cumin seeds. Once the mustard seeds pop, add to the rasam.
A few sprigs of coriander	♦ Stir well; add coriander and serve.

Suggested composition

Rice
Rasam
Paruppu usili
Salad

Mix the *paruppu usili* with rice with a dash of ghee and spoon on the *rasam* little by little as you eat. Alternatively, mix rice and *rasam* together and combine *paruppu usili* with it as a side dish.

Mulligatawny Soup

Ingredients	Method
2 tbs coriander seeds 1 tbs cumin 1 tsp fenugreek 1 cinnamon stick (about 1")	In a skillet, dry-roast ingredients listed alongside until they release a pleasing aroma. ♦ Grind in a blender or processor to a powder.
1/2 c toordal A pinch of turmeric powder	♦ Wash and cook toordal (see Notes on page 10), adding a pinch of turmeric, to a soft consistency; mash to a puree.
2 tbs ghee 2 medium onions, peeled and chopped 2 carrots, diced small 1 tsp fresh ginger, finely chopped 2 cloves of garlic	♦ Heat oil or ghee in a saucepan; saute onion, carrot, ginger and garlic until the onion is translucent. Be careful not to over-saute.
3 large tomatoes, chopped 1 1/2 c water	♦ Add sauteed ingredients to the cooked dal along with powdered spices, tomatoes and water, and cook in a saucepan, mashing the tomatoes well.

Mulligatawny Soup - contd.

Ingredients	Method
	♦ Once mixed together, blend everything well in a processor and strain.
1/3 c thick coconut milk Lemon juice to taste 1 1/2 tsp salt	♦ Return it to saucepan and heat gently with coconut milk, salt and lemon juice to taste. ♦ Heat until the liquid reaches boiling point and begins to foam.
A few sprigs of coriander	♦ Garnish with coriander and serve.

Mysore Rasam

Ingredients	Method
1/4 c Toordal 1 c water	Cook toor dal (see Notes on page 10). Mash well and add water. Set aside.
A small lemon sized tamarind or 1 tsp tamarind paste	♦ Prepare 1 1/2 c tamarind water in a pan (see Notes on page 12).
1 1/2 tsp salt 1/2 tsp turmeric powder 1/2 tsp rasam powder	♦ Add salt, turmeric and rasam powder, and boil over medium heat.
2 tsp coriander seeds 1 tsp channa dal 5 or 6 pepper corns 1/2 tsp cumin 1 small dry red chili 2 tsp shredded coconut 1 tbs ghee	♦ In a heated skillet, fry the ingredients listed alongside and grind to a coarse paste. Add to the boiling tamarind water and stir well to prevent lumps.
1/4 tsp hing 1 tsp brown sugar	♦ Add hing and brown sugar.

Mysore Rasam - contd.

Ingredients	Method
1 c tomatoes, chopped	♦ After boiling for 5 more minutes over medium heat, add tomatoes and dal water. ♦ Remove from heat when the liquid starts to foam.
2 tbs ghee or melted butter 1 tsp mustard seeds	♦ Season with mustard seeds popped in heated ghee.
A few sprigs of coriander, chopped	♦ Add coriander and serve.

Note: This rasam will be slightly thicker than other varieties on account of the ground spices.

Lentil and Tomato Soup

Ingredients	Method
1/2 c toordal	Cook toordal (see Notes on page 10). Remove and mash well.
2 tsp ghee 1 tsp mustard seeds 2 small green chilies, chopped 1 onion, finely chopped	♦ In a skillet, heat ghee and pop mustard seeds. Add chilies and onion and saute.
1/2 tsp turmeric 1 tsp salt 1 c water 3 or 4 large, ripe tomatoes, chopped	♦ Add to the cooked dal along with water, turmeric and salt. ♦ Add tomatoes and bring to a boil. Allow mixture to boil for 5 minutes until well-blended.
1 tsp heavy cream 1 tsp finely chopped coriander	♦ When the soup begins to foam, remove from heat. Add cream and coriander.
1 tsp lemon juice	♦ Let stand for 10 minutes; add lemon juice and serve.

Side Vegetables

The side vegetable, a dry preparation, helps to give a balance to the meal, both for visual effect and from the point of view of taste and nutrition.

For instance, if the vegetable gravy has a combination of vegetables, like *Aviyal, Poritha Kuzhambu* or *Poritha Koottu*, you could go for a crispy, crunchy preparation (crunchy potatoes, okra, eggplant, yam or raw banana fry). If on the other hand, the main gravy dish is low on vegetable content, you could increase the nutritional value of the meal by including a lightly prepared 'green vegetable' like beans.

The effect of a speciality preparation like *Paruppu Usili* can be best brought out by combining it with the tangy flavour of *Mor Kuzhambu, Vattal Kuzhambu or Milagu Kuzhambu.*

"Fortune smiles on the host
who plays host with a smile."
- Tirukkural - chapter on Hospitality -

Side Vegetables

Eggplant Fry
(with powdered spices)

Ingredients	Method
2 tsp coriander seeds 1tsp urad dal 1 tsp channa dal 2 small red chilies 1 tbs oil	Saute the ingredients listed alongside in oil until golden brown and grind coarsely. Set aside.
1 large eggplant (1/2 lb. or 200 - 250 gms.)	♦ Thinly slice eggplant and cut each slice into 2" pieces. Place them in salt water to prevent discolouring.
3 tbs oil 1/2 tsp mustard seeds 1 tsp salt	♦ Pop mustard seeds in oil. Add eggplant and salt. Saute for about 5-8 minutes, stirring from time to time.
	♦ Add the ground ingredients and simmer for about 5 more minutes. Serve.

Eggplant with Onions

Ingredients	Method
2 c chopped eggplant (tender)	Cut eggplant into 1/2" pieces and place in salt water for 10 minutes; drain completely.
3 tbs oil 2 tbs ghee 1tsp mustard seeds 1 tsp urad dal 2 tbs chana dal 3 tbs chopped cashew nuts	♦ Heat oil and ghee and add mustard seeds. Once they pop, add rest of the ingredients listed alongside.
2 c onion, finely chopped 2 small green chilies, chopped	♦ As the nuts and dals get partially browned, add chilies, and after a few seconds, onions, and saute. As the onion becomes translucent, add the drained eggplant; cook on very low heat for 8-10 minutes, stirring from time to time.
1 tsp salt 1/2 tsp turmeric	♦ Add salt and turmeric.
1 tbs lemon juuice 1 tbs finely chopped coriander	♦ Add lemon juice and coriander. Stir until everything is well blended.
	♦ Serve with rice or *chappatis*.

Eggplant Bartha

Ingredients	Method
1 large eggplant (1/2 lb. or 200-250 gms.)	Wash eggplant, cut off the stem and make a lengthwise slit. Bake at 375º (appro. 1/2 hour) until the skin is nearly charred, turning over frequently for even baking. (My preference is to roast it on a gas range. See page 101).
4 tbs oil 1/2 tsp mustard seeds	♦ Place the eggplant under cool water and remove the skin. Mash and set aside. ♦ Pop mustard seeds in heated oil.
1 tsp coriander powder 1 tsp cumin powder 1 1/2 tsp chili powder 1/4 tsp ground black pepper A pinch of turmeric 1cup onion, finely chopped	♦ Add remaining spices and onion. Saute until the spices are thoroughly absorbed.
1 c tomato juice 1 tsp salt A few sprigs of coriander	♦ Add the mashed eggplant, salt and tomato juice. ♦ Simmer, stirring occasionally for about 10 minutes. ♦ Garnish with coriander and serve.

Dry Red Kidney Beans

Two 8 oz. cans of red kidney beans	Wash and drain red kidney beans in a colander.
2 tbs oil 1 tsp mustard seeds 2 tsp urad dal 2 small, dry red chilies, chopped 1 tsp finely chopped cashews	♦ In a skillet, heat oil ; add mustard seeds, urad dal, red chilies and cashews. When the mustard seeds have popped and the dal has turned golden brown, add kidney beans and stir for about three minutes.
1/4 tsp salt 1/4 tsp curry powder* A few curry leaves 1/8 tsp hing	♦ Add salt, curry powder, curry leaves, hing, and mix well before serving.

Note A real quick-and-easy recipe. Make sure you buy a good brand. Canned organic, preservative-free beans are available in most grocery stores.
The red kidney beans in this recipe can be replaced with chick peas. If doing so, add 2 tbs shredded coconut at the end for additional flavour.
* For alternative to store-bought curry powder, see recipe on page 158.

Okra Fry

1 1/2 c green tender okra, sliced into small pieces 1/2 tsp salt 1/2 tsp turmeric 1 tsp chili powder	Mix salt, turmeric and chili powder with okra; let stand for 10 minutes.
3 tbs oil 1 tsp mustard seeds	♦ Heat oil in a skillet and pop mustard seeds. ♦ Add the spiced okra mix. Stir thoroughly and cook covered for 5 minutes. Reduce heat and continue to cook, stirring occasionally. ♦ If the okra becomes too dry, add a little more oil. You can either saute the okra until brown and slightly crispy, or leave it green, but well-cooked. The choice is yours. **Note** You could add a tbs yoghurt to the marinade (step 1) to take away the slimy texture of the okra.

Green Beans stir-fry

Ingredients	Method
1 c green beans, chopped 1/2 tsp salt	Wash the beans. Drain well and add salt.
1 tbs oil 1 tsp ghee	♦ In a skillet, heat oil and ghee (or butter).
1 tsp mustard seeds 2 tbs urad dal	♦ Add mustard seeds and urad dal. ♦ As the dal gets browned, reduce heat to low and add the beans.
A pinch of baking soda	♦ Add a pinch of baking soda and stir well.
2 tbs shredded coconut	♦ Cook on low heat for 10 minutes and add shredded coconut just before serving.

Note: All varieties of green beans, as also cabbabge can be cooked in this method.

Crunchy Potatoes

Ingredients	Method
3 medium potatoes	Boil potatoes until soft.
1/2 tsp salt 1/4 tsp turmeric 1 tsp chili powder 1/4 tsp hing	♦ Cut into cubes and add salt, turmeric, hing and chili powder; let stand for 10 minutes.
5 tsp oil 1 tsp mustard seeds	♦ Heat oil in a skillet and pop mustard seeds. ♦ Add the spiced potatoes and mix well. ♦ Cook on low heat, stirring occasionally until the potatoes are golden brown and crunchy on the outside. Adjust salt. Serve.
2 onions, chopped (optional)	**Note:** Onions may also be added to this recipe. If so, saute two small, finely chopped onions first and set aside. Add after the potatoes have turned golden brown and crisp, and mix well.

Potato & Carrot Vadakkal

(Potato & Carrot fry)

Ingredients	Method
3 medium potatoes 3 medium carrots	Wash and dice potatoes and carrots small; drain thoroughly
1 tsp salt 1/4 tsp turmeric 1 1/2 tsp chili powder 1/4 tsp hing	♦ Add salt, turmeric, chili powder and hing.Mix well and let stand for 5 minutes
4 tbs oil 1 tsp mustard seeds	♦ In a Skillet, heat oil and pop mustard seeds. ♦ Add carrots and potatoes, and cook on low heat, stirring occasionally for 6-8 minutes. Allow the vegetables to brown. Serve.

Note: Two small onions may be added for more flavour. If desired, chop and saute onions separately and add to carrot and potato mixture

Potato Onion Fry

Ingredients	Method
2 large potatoes (appro. 1 lb)	Boil, peel and cut the potatoes into chunks.
3 tbs oil 2 tsp mustard seeds 2 tsp urad dal 1 tsp channa dal	♦ In a deep skillet or wok, heat oil; add mustard seeds, urad dal and channa dal.
2 green chilies, chopped 2 tsp ginger, finely chopped 2 medium onions (appro. 1/2 lb), chopped	♦ As the mustard seeds begin to crackle and the dals start browning, add chilies and ginger, and saute for a few seconds ♦ Add onion and saute until translucent.
1 1/2 tsp salt 1 tsp turmeric	♦ Add potatoes, salt and turmeric, and stir. Cook for 3 minutes on low to medium heat until well-blended.
3 tsp chickpea flour (besan) 1/2 c water	♦ Stir in chickpea flour dissolved in water and cook for 2 more minutes .
1/4 tsp hing A few sprigs curry leaves	♦ Add hing and hurry leaves before removing. The final consistency is semi-liquid.

Note: An ideal accompaniment for Indian breads, especially *pooris*.

Potato Podimas

Mashed Potatoes (Indian style)

Ingredients	Method
4 medium potatoes	Boil potatoes until soft.
1/4 c cooked green peas 1/2 tsp salt 2 small green chilies, chopped	♦ Peel once cooled and mash coarsely with a spatula or spoon. ♦ Add salt and cooked green peas. Mix in the chilies.
2 tbs oil or ghee 1 tsp mustard seeds 1 tsp urad dal 1 tsp chana dal 2 tbs cashews, chopped 1 tsp ginger, grated	♦ In a skillet, heat oil or ghee and pop mustard seeds. Add rest of the ingredients listed alongside. Allow them to brown. ♦ Add the potato-peas mixture and stir until well- blended.
1/4 tsp hing A few curry leaves A few sprigs of coriander 1 tsp lemon juice	♦ Add hing, curry leaves, coriander and lemon juice. Stir for half a minute.

Comment: Makes a very good side dish for any of the vegetable gravy - rice combination.

Taroroot (Colacasia) Fry

Ingredients	Method
1 lb. Taroroot (1/2 kg.)	Wash taroroot thoroughly 3-4 times. Boil in clear water until soft. Peel. Unlike potatoes, cooked tarorrot will be soft and a bit sticky. Cut into appro. 1" square piece, 1/2" thick .
1 tsp salt 1 tsp turmeric 1 1/2 tsp chili powder 1/4 tsp hing 1 tbs chickpea flour (Besan)	♦ Place the cut pieces in a bowl, add salt, turmeric, chili powder, hing and chickpea flour. Mix well and let stand for 10 minutes (the longer the better)
4-5 tbs oil 1-2 tbs of butter or ghee 1 tsp mustard seeds	♦ Heat oil in a heavy-bottomed wok and pop mustard seeds. ♦ Add the marinated vegetables and stir. ♦ Saute on low heat, stirring occasionally to allow the tarroroot to get brown. Add butter or ghee and keep covered towards the end for extra flavour and crispiness.

Note: Indian and Pakistani stores are likely to have this vegetable (known as Arbi). Stores or market stands that stock vegetables from Kenya are also a good bet.

Paruppu Usili

(Steamed lentils with vegetables)

Ingredients	Method
1/4 c toor dal 1/2 c channa dal	Soak the two dals separately for about 2 hours. Wash the soaked dals twice and drain completely.
1/2 tsp salt 2 small, dry red chilies, finely chopped	♦ Grind the dal in a blender with salt and red chilies to a smooth paste, using very little water.
1 - 1 1/2 c green beans or cabbage, chopped	♦ Wash and steam either green beans or cabbage with 1/4 tsp salt. Set aside. ♦ Grease a stainless steel plate, spread the ground paste about 1/4" thick and steam for 8 minutes. (If in a pressure cooker, make sure that you place the plate at a sufficient height, so that it can be taken out easily. If you are cooking rice at the same time, the plate, of course, could be placed on top of it)

Paruppu Usili - contd.

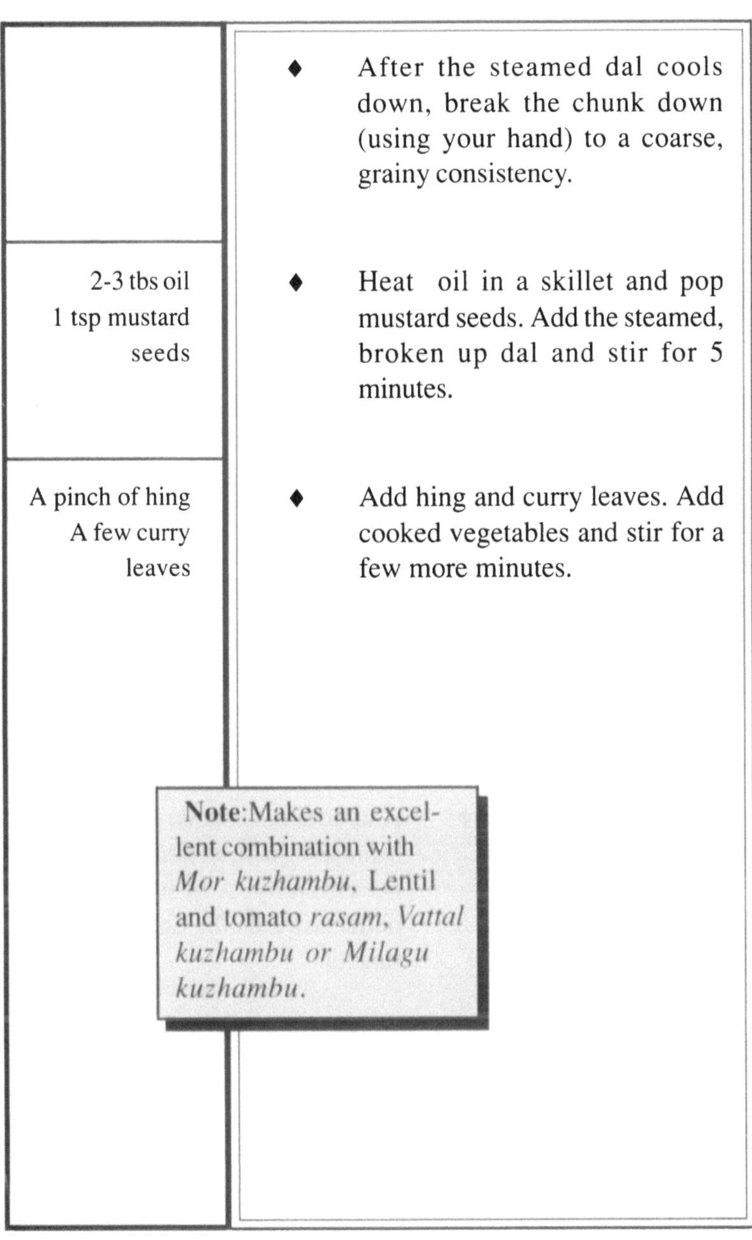

	♦ After the steamed dal cools down, break the chunk down (using your hand) to a coarse, grainy consistency.
2-3 tbs oil 1 tsp mustard seeds	♦ Heat oil in a skillet and pop mustard seeds. Add the steamed, broken up dal and stir for 5 minutes.
A pinch of hing A few curry leaves	♦ Add hing and curry leaves. Add cooked vegetables and stir for a few more minutes.

Note:Makes an excellent combination with *Mor kuzhambu*, Lentil and tomato *rasam*, *Vattal kuzhambu or Milagu kuzhambu*.

Raw Banana Fry

Ingredients	Method
2 c raw banana, peeled and cut into 1/2" square pieces, 1/4" thick	For convenience, cut up the banana into 2 or 3 bits, and work on each piece separately. ♦ As you cut the banana, drop the pieces into a bowl of water to prevent it from turning black.
1tsp salt 1/4 tsp turmeric powder	♦ Steam the banana, adding salt and turmeric.
3-4 tsp oil 1 tsp mustard seeds 2 tsp urad dal 1 dry, red chili, chopped 1/4 tsp hing 3-4 curry leaves 1 tsp butter	♦ On medium heat, pour oil into a heavy-bottomed wok and pop mustard seeds. Add rest of the ingredients and fry until the dal turns golden brown. ♦ Add cooked banana. Cook for 5 minutes on low heat, stirring occasionally. Adjust salt. Add butter towards the end for extra flavour.

Comment: Bananas with white flesh inside are the soft variety and take less time to cook. The other variety which is somewhat pink inside takes more time.
Pre-cooking the banana reduces the quantity of oil. The recipe alongside is a variation.

Raw Banana Fry

(with powdered masala)

3 raw bananas, washed, peeled and cut into thin slices	Set the slices of banana in water as you cut them. ♦ Drain the water completely and wipe the banana pieces dry with a towel.
4-5 tbs oil 1 tsp mustard seeds 1 1/2 tsp curry powder 1/4 tsp turmeric 1/4 tsp hing 1-2 tbs butter	♦ Heat oil in a large nonstick wok on medium heat and pop mustard seeds. Add the rest of the ingredients and the banana slices. ♦ Keep the pan covered initially for 5 minutes. Allow plenty of time for the banana to get roasted gently on slow heat. ♦ See that the vegetable does not stick to the pan or get burnt. Add more oil or butter, if necessary.

Comment: Obviously not a stir-and-mix recipe. But the result is so delicious that it is worth every second you put into it.

For recipe for curry powder, refer to page 158. You may also use chili powder (1 tsp) as an alternative.

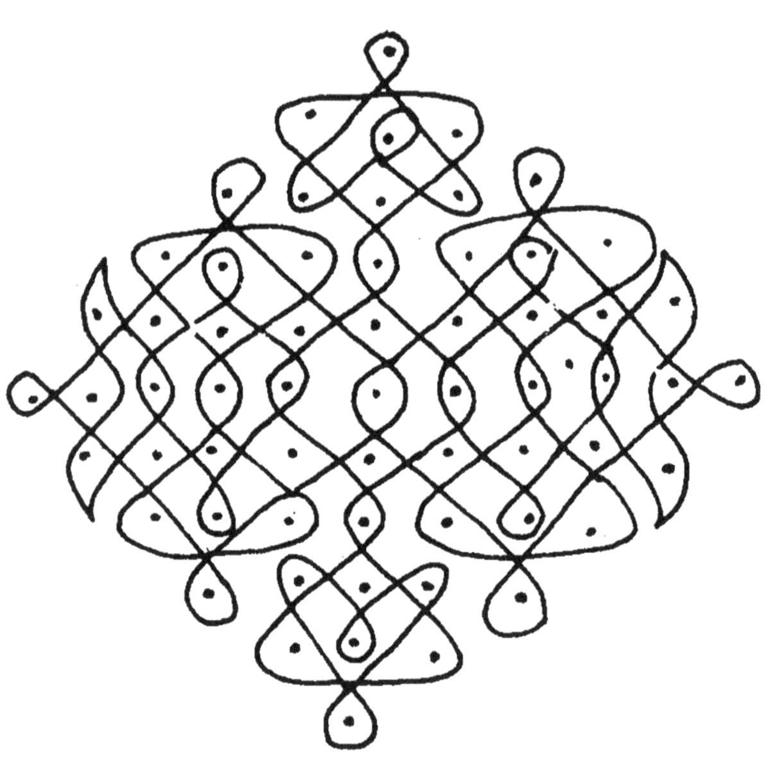

Chutneys

Chutneys are meant as accompaniments to pep up a meal with, but it is sometimes difficult to keep children - and oneself - from making a meal out of them.

They are either vegetable-based (chayote, coriander, mint, eggplant, coconut) or lentil-based, and ground together with chilies, asafoetida and other condiments to get the taste buds tingling. Versatile as they are, they lend themselves to be mixed both with rice and Indian breads.

A few dry powders (*sambar*, *rasam*, *curry*) included in this chapter do not serve the purpose of accompaniments but are spice-mixtures used in the preparation of certain vegetable gravies or side vegetables. In South Indian homes, they are normally prepared in large quantities, as they keep well for a long time without refrigeration.

Milagai podi (chili-dal mixture) is a speciality-accompaniment created exclusively to go with *idlis* or *dosais*, but you can also make a difference to an ordinary buttered toast by sprinkling a little of the powder over it.

Chutneys

"To have no guests is to experience want in the midst of plenty; such poverty belongs to fools."
- Tirukkural, chapter on Hospitality -

Green Coriander (cilantro) Chutney

Ingredients	Method
2 tbs oil 1 tsp mustard seeds 2 tsp urad dal 2 small red chilies 1/4 tsp hing	Heat oil in a skillet. Pop mustard seeds over low heat. Add urad dal and chilies. When the dal is browned, add hing; remove from heat after 3 seconds. ♦ Place all the fried ingredients in a blender and grind to a coarse powder.
1/2 tsp salt A marble-sized chunk of tamarind (or 1/2 tsp tamarind paste) 1 c coriander leaves,chopped fine (no stems and tightly packed) 2 - 3 tbs water	♦ Add salt, tamarind and coriander, and continue to grind, adding water little by little.
1tsp jaggery (or brown sugar)	♦ Add jaggery (or sugar) and grind briefly to a semi-solid consistency. **Note:** The tricky part is the seasoning. The oil should be on low heat. Keep the ingredients ready at hand. Over-heating the mustard seeds will spoil the entire dish.

Chayote Chutney

Ingredients	Method
2 medium-sized tender chayote	Wash, peel and and dice chayote into 1/2" cubes.
2 tbs oil	♦ Saute in oil until slightly browned and set aside.
1 tbs oil 1 tsp mustard seeds 2 tbs urad dal 1 tsp channa dal 2 small red chilies A pinch of hing	♦ In the same skillet, heat oil and pop mustard seeds; add dals, red chilies and hing, and fry to a golden brown. Grind to a powder in a blender.
1/2 tsp salt A marble-sized chunk of tamarind or 1/4 tsp of tamarind paste A few sprigs of coriander	♦ To the blended mix, add sauteed chayote, salt, tamarind and coriander, and grind to a coarse consistency. Serve with hot rice, adding a dash of ghee or melted butter.

Note: Also makes an excellent spread over bread.

Suggested composition:
Rice
Chayote chutney
Any of the *rasams*
Green beans fry

Mint Chutney

3 tbs oil
1 tsp mustard seeds
2 tbs urad dal
3 or 4 small red chilies
1/8 tsp fenugreek
1/4 tsp hing

In a skillet, heat oil. Over low heat, pop mustard seeds. Add urad dal, fenugreek and red chilies and fry until browned. Add hing, and after 3 seconds, remove the fried mixture from the skillet.

1 c tender mint leaves (without stems and tightly packed), washed and dried

- In the same skillet, saute mint leaves for a minute or two.

1/4 c coriander, chopped
1/2 lemon-sized chunk of tamarind
1 tsp salt

- Powder the fried ingredients in a blender; add mint, coriander, salt and tamarind, and grind to a smooth consistency with just 1 - 2 tbs water.

Note: Goes well with hot basmati rice. When mixing with rice, add a tsp toasted sesame oil or ghee. Makes an excellent spread for sandwiches or over toasts.

Mint chutney

(Sauce form)

1 1/2 oz. mint leaves

1/2 - 3/4 c coriander, chopped

1 tsp lemon juice

1/2 tsp cumin

2-3 green chilies, chopped

1 tsp salt

Place all the ingredients in a food processor and grind, adding water slowly to form a thick sauce.

Note This is a spicy chutney and makes an excellent dipping sauce for *samosas*, *pakoras*, etc.

Paruppu Tuvaiyal

(Lentils chutney)

Ingredients	Method
1/2 tsp oil 1/2 c Toordal 1/2 c chana dal	In a heavy-bottomed skillet, roast the two dals separately in oil over medium heat.
1 or 2 small red chilies	♦ Add chilies a few seconds before taking the dals off heat.
	♦ When the dals have cooled down a little (grinding is easier when they are still warm), grind to a fine powder in a mixer.
1/4 tsp salt 4 tbs shredded coconut	♦ Add salt and shredded coconut, and give it another spin.
1-2 tbs water	♦ Add water and blend to a smooth, thick consistency.

Note: This chutney is normally eaten mixed with rice. Add a dash of melted butter to bring out the flavour.

Suggested combination :
Rice-*Tuvaiyal* mixture
Rasam or *Vattal kuzhambu*
Green vegetables

Comment: Grandmas often refer to this combination as the humblest of fares - "even if I can't give you a feast, I am still good enough for *Paruppu Tuvaiyal* and *Vattal kuzhambu*." But it is a meal worth walking miles for. A fact that grandmas know only too well.

Coconut chutney

Ingredients	Method
1 c shredded coconut 4-5 sprigs of coriander 3 medium green chilies 3/4 tsp salt 1/2 tsp tamarind 2 tbs dahlia	In a blender, place ingredients listed alongside and grind for a minute or two.
2 - 3 tbs water	♦ Add water and grind to a smooth paste. Remove into a serving bowl.
2 tbs oil 1 tsp mustard seeds 1 small red chili, cut into small pieces A few curry leaves	♦ Heat oil in a small skillet or a mini wok. Over medium heat, add mustard seeds and red chilies together. When the mustard seeds start to pop, add the contents to the ground chutney. ♦ Serve with *idli*, *dosai* or *vadai*. **Comment:** This chutney tastes best when made with fresh coconut.

Milagai Podi

(Chili & Dal Powder)

2 tbs sesame seeds	In a dry skillet, roast the sesame seeds and set aside.
2 tbs oil 1 tsp mustard seeds 1/2 c urad dal 6 small red chilies 1/2 tsp hing a marble-sized chunk of tamarind	♦ In the same skillet, heat oil and pop mustard seeds. ♦ Add dal, chilies and hing, and stir until the dal gets browned; add tamarind and remove from heat after a few seconds.
1 tsp salt 1 tsp brown sugar	♦ In a blender, grind the roasted sesame seeds first and remove. Grind the fried ingredients along with salt to a coarse powder. Add brown sugar and powdered sesame seeds, and blend for a few more seconds.

Note: This is an ideal accomapaniment for *idli* and *dosai*. Add a tsp of sesame, vegetable oil or ghee to a couple of spoons of the powder.
As a dry powder, it can be stored in an air-tight jar for up to one month.

Comment: This is a relatively mild recipe. Increase the quantity of chilies, if you would like it more pungent.

Sambar Powder

Ingredients	Method
2 c coriander seeds 1 tbs whole black pepper 2 tbs fenugreek 1/2 c toor dal 1/2 c channa dal 2 tbs mustard seeds 1 tbs turmeric powder	In a heated skillet, dry-roast ingredients listed alongside for 5-8 minutes, making sure not to scorch the spices. Remove from skillet.
1 tbs oil 2 c whole dry red chilies, tightly packed	♦ To the same hot skillet, add oil and red chilies. Remove from heat, but leave the chilies in for approximately 10 minutes to get roasted in residual heat of skillet. (This is important, as over-frying would spoil the colour as well as the flavour.) ♦ Grind everything together to a fine powder.

Note: Stored in a dry, air-tight jar, this will keep for a long time..
Apart from *Sambar*, you could also use this to spice up any stew-like vegetable preparation you may invent!

Rasam Powder

2 c coriander seeds
1/2 c whole dried red chilies
1/4 c channa dal
1/2 c toor dal
2 tbs whole black pepper
2 tbs cumin
3 tbs turmeric powder

Dry-roast the ingredients in a heated skillet.

- Using a blender or food processor, grind to a powder.
- Stored in a dry, air-tight jar, the powder keeps for a long time.

Curry Powder

Ingredients	Method
2 tbs oil 1/2 c coriander seeds 1/2 c channa dal 10-12 small red chilies 1/4 c urad dal 1/4 c shredded coconut	Saute the ingredients in oil. ♦ Grind to a coarse powder in a blender and keep in an air-tight jar. ♦ This powder is used in the preparation of shallow-fried vegetables like eggplant or raw banana. **Note:** *Curry* in recent times has been elevated to international prominence. In many parts of India and in the West, it is celebrated in books and restaurants in a sauce form.In most South Indian homes, however, it is known in an entirely different *avatar,* as a dry vegetable. **The curry powder in this recipe is generally used only for dry, but spicy and roasted vegetable preparations.**

Pachidis

(Yoghurt-based side dishes)

All meals in South India, whether daily fare or feast, with family or friends, by rain or sunshine, always end with yoghurt. *Tayir sadam* - rice mixed with yoghurt - along with a vegetable is a standard packed lunch for school-going children.

It has been mentioned elsewhere in the book that even at a wedding feast, *Tayir sadam* will be served last - *after* the sweet dish. The rationale behind this peculiarity among South Indians is that yoghurt is an antidote to acidity and therefore has a settling effect on the stomach; yoghurt also serves as a cleaning agent for the palate (like the Chinese tea during a chinese meal) besides being a very good milk product, better than milk itself.

The recipes in this section are flavoured and spiced up yoghurt which can accompany a meal right through, saving you the anxiety of having to wait until the end!

Pachidis

"We gathered wealth and lost will be the refrain of regret of those who never entertained guests."
- Tirukkural, chapter on Hospitality -

Chayote Raita

Ingredients	Method
1 small, tender chayote	Wash and peel chayote (also called chow chow) before grating it.
1/3 tsp salt	♦ Add salt and set aside for 5-10 minutes. Drain.
1 tbs oil 1 tsp mustard seeds 1 green chili, chopped fine 1/2 tsp cumin	♦ Pop mustard seeds in heated oil, and add cumin and chilies. Add to the chayote.
1 c thick yoghurt A few sprigs of coriander	♦ Just before serving, add the yoghurt and stir well. Garnish with coriander.

Note An excellent addition to any meal. You could also try it as a dip.

Cucumber Raita

Ingredients	Method
2 small cucumbers	Peel, seed, and cut cucumber into 1/2" cubes or grate them. If they are very tender, the seeds need not be removed.
1/2 tsp salt	♦ Add salt and set aside for 5 minutes. Drain, squeezing excess liquid from cucumbers.
1 tbs oil 1/2 tsp mustard seeds 1/2 tsp urad dal (optional)	♦ Season with mustard seeds and urad dal in oil. (see Notes on page 11).
1 c plain yoghurt A few sprigs of coriander	♦ Add yoghurt just before serving and garnish with chopped coriander.

Note Shredded carrots and/or tomatoes may also be added to this recipe for additional colour and taste. Be sure to increase the yoghurt proportionally. The yoghurt should be thick, but not creamy.

Eggplant Raita

Ingredients	Method
1 or 2 medium eggplants	Oil the eggplants and bake at 375° until the skin is nearly charred, making sure to turn them occasionally for even cooking. ♦ Under cool running water, peel the skin.
1/2 tsp salt	♦ Mash eggplant coarsely with a ladle or spoon. Mix in salt
2 tsp oil 1/2 tsp mustard seeds 1/2 tsp urad dal (optional)	♦ Season with mustard seeds and urad dal (see Notes on page 11).
1 c plain yoghurt A few sprigs of coriander leaves	♦ Add yoghurt just before serving. Garnish with coriander.

Okra Raita

Ingredients	Method
10-12 okra	Wash okra and dry with a towel. Cut into very thin slices.
2 tbs oil 1/2 tsp mustard seeds	♦ In a skillet, heat oil and pop mustard seeds.
1/2 tsp salt 1 very small green chili, chopped (optional)	♦ Add okra, salt and chili. Keep stirring until the okra turns golden brown. Set aside.
1 c yoghurt A few sprigs of coriander	♦ Add yoghurt just before serving to keep the okra crisp. It is preferable to keep the yoghurt in lumps rather than stiring it to a smooth consistency. Chopped coriander makes a nice garnish.

Note: With tender vegetables like okra, cucumber, tomatoes and carrots, it is preferable not to add any other spices in order to preserve the natural flavours.

Potato Raita

Ingredients	Method
2 or 3 small potatos 1/3 tsp salt	Boil potatos and mash coarsely. Add salt.
1 tbs ghee 1/2 tsp mustard seeds 1 tsp urad dal 1 or 2 small green chilies, chopped	♦ Season with mustard seeds, chilies and urad dal (see Notes on page 11).
1 c thick plain yoghurt A few sprigs of coriander	♦ Add chopped coriander., Add yoghurt just before serving. ♦ It is as tasty as it is simple.

Tomato-Cucumber Raita

Ingredients	Method
1 big, firm, red tomato	The tomato should be firm and not over-ripe. Cut into small pieces. Set aside.
1/4 c cucumber (peeled and cut very small) Salt to taste	♦ Mix salt with cucumber and set aside to allow the water to collect. After 5 minutes, squeeze out the water and place in a mixing bowl.
2 tsp oil 1/2 tsp mustard seeds 2 green chilies, cut very small	♦ In a small skillet, heat oil and add mustard seeds. ♦ As the seeds start to pop, add chopped green chilies. After 10 - 15 seconds, add the garnish to the cucumber.
One 8 oz. carton yoghurt 1 tbs coriander leaves, chopped	♦ Just before serving, add yoghurt to the seasoneed cucumber. Mix in the tomato pieces and coriander.

Onion-Tomato Raita

Ingredients	Method
1/2 c tomatoes, cut small	Wash and cut tomatoes into small pieces. Leave aside the soft portions to be used later in soups or *rasam*.
1/4 c onion	♦ Dice onion; set aside.
1 c thick yoghurt	♦ Keep a mixing bowl ready with thick yoghurt.
1 tbs oil 1 tsp mustard seeds 4-5 small pieces of green chilies	♦ Heat oil in a small pan or wok. Add mustard seeds. ♦ As they begin to pop, add green chilies. After 10 seconds, add the mix to the yoghurt.
A few sprigs of coriander, chopped	♦ Mix in coriander. Keep refrigerated.
Salt to taste 2 tbs sour cream	♦ Just before serving, add chopped onions, tomatoes and salt, and stir gently. Mix in sour cream.

Note If the salt is added earlier, it tends to make the raita watery.

Sweet Dishes

Sweet dishes are - literally - fit for the Gods . For the Hindu, Gods do not live in a remote heaven but are quite accessible. Therefore, even their particular taste in sweets is an established fact and regularly indulged! For instance, *modakas*, rice dumplings with a filling of coconut and jaggery are prepared for Lord Ganesh , *seedais* on Lord Krishna's birthday, *laddus* and *sakkarai pongal* for Lord Venkateswara and so on. And all of them like *payasam*, a milk-based liquid preparation.

Although *payasam* is reserved for a special occasion such as a festival, a birthday or for an honoured or dear guest, in traditional homes cooked rice and a bowl of sweetened milk would be offered at the family shrine everyday.

The following are just a few drops from the 'ksheer sagara' or milky ocean.

Sweet Dishes

"... do you know the recipe for honeycombs?"
- Pablo Neruda

"In Madras a long time since,
I saw a sugary pyramid,
a tower of confectionery -
one level after another,
and in the construction, rubies,
and other blushing delights,
medieval and yellow.

Someone dirtied his hands
to cook up so much sweetness."

- Pablo Neruda (from the poem 'Sweetness, always')

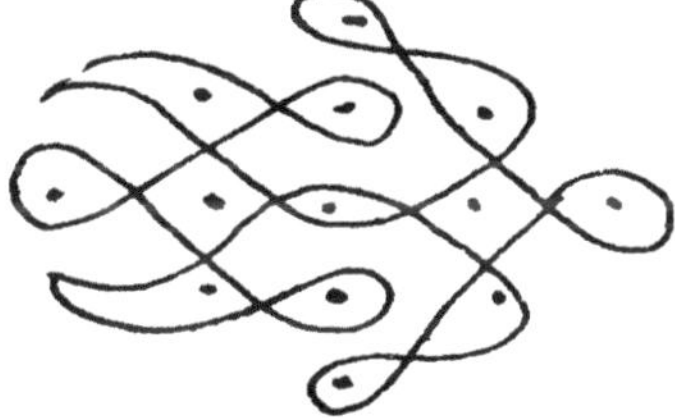

Rava (Semolina) Payasam

Ingredients	Method
1/4 c ghee 3 tbs cashews, in halves or quarters	In a heavy skillet, fry cashews in 2 tbs ghee over low heat. Remove when golden to dark brown and set aside.
2 tbs golden raisins	♦ Heat raisins similarly and add to cashew pieces.
1/2 c rava (semolina)	♦ In the ghee left over in the pan (you might need to add another tbs), roast semolina until it turns light brown and the raw smell disappears.
2 c water	♦ Bring water to a boil and add slowly to the roasted rava in the skillet over medium heat, stirring constantly. ♦ Reduce heat and keep stirring on low heat until the mixture thickens.

Rava Payasam - contd.

Ingredients	Method
2 c sugar A few strands of saffron soaked in milk or A pinch of saffron powder	♦ As it thickens, slowly add sugar and then the saffron milk.
3 c milk	♦ Add milk and heat for 3 minutes.
1/4 tbs cardamom powder	♦ Add cardamom powder, cashews and raisins. Remove from heat.

Note: Although the steps seem many, this is a quick-to-make sweet dish. Serve as dessert.

Milk Payasam

(Kerala style)

2 tbs ghee 1/3 c basmati rice	In a heavy-bottomed saucepan, heat ghee and saute rice for 2 minutes. Remove from heat.
1/2 c of milk 1/2 c water	♦ In a large container, mix milk and water; add rice and cook.
3 1/2 c milk	♦ Remove and mash well with a ladle; simmer in a saucepan, adding milk every 5 minutes for another 20 minutes or so until the entire amount is used up.
2 c sugar	♦ Add sugar and simmer for another 5 minutes.
A few strands of saffron soaked in 1 tbs milk 1 tsp cardamom powder	♦ Add saffron-milk mixture and cardamom. ♦ If you feel that the consistency is too thick, add 1/2 - 1 c milk.

Milk Payasam - contd.

2 tbs cashew nuts or 1 tbs raisins or both (optional) 1 tbs ghee	♦ As an option, you can garnish with cashews and raisins, sauteed in ghee.

Note: A basic sweet dish known in many parts of the world. The saffron and the cardamom perhaps give it the Indian touch.
I know of adventurous spirits who add date syrup at the end. Up to you!

Moong Dal Payasam

Ingredients	Method
1/4 c moong dal 1/4 c channa dal	In a skillet, dry-roast dals to a golden brown until the raw smell disappears. ♦ Wash thoroughly in water.
2 c milk 1 c water	♦ Cook the dals in milk and water to a soft consistency in an open pan.
1/2 c shredded coconut	♦ In the meantime, grind coconut to a smooth paste and add to the cooked dal. Alternatively, add 1/2 c coconut milk.
1 1/2 c powdered jaggery (see Notes on page 9) 1/2 tsp ground cardamom	♦ Add jaggery and boil for 5 minutes. Add cardamom and serve.
Optional: 1 tbs cashews **or** 2 tbs shredded coconut	♦ Can be garnished either with cashews or shredded coconut, sauteed in a tbs ghee.

Carrot Halwa

Ingredients	Method
2 c carrots, peeled and diced 1/2 c water	Add water to carrots and cook (no need to add water if using pressure cooker).
1/4 c cashews	♦ Powder cashews coarsely by pounding (preferably not in a processor). ♦ Drain the water from the cooked carrots (Use the water for soup or rasam) and puree with a ladle. (Using a blender will make the texture too smooth.)
1 1/2 c sugar 1/2 c ghee	♦ Using a heavy-bottomed skillet or pan and on low heat, mix the carrot puree with sugar. After about 5 minutes, add the powdered cashews. As the mix begins to thicken, slowly mix in warm ghee.
4-5 strands of saffron soaked in 1 tbs milk A pinch of cardamom powder	♦ Add saffron and cardamom powder and continue to stir. Remove from heat when the halwa does not stick to your finger or to the side of the skillet.

Sakkarai Pongal

(Rice cooked with milk and jaggery)

Ingredients	Method
1/4 c moong dal	In a skillet dry-roast moong dal for 3 minutes, stirring constantly until the raw smell disappears.
1 c rice 2 1/2 c water	♦ Wash the dry-roasted dal and raw rice together; cook in a pressure cooker to a smooth consistency by cooking for 10 minutes longer than usual. If not using a pressure cooker, use 3 1/2 c water to cook.
1 to 1 1/2 c milk	♦ Remove from pan/cooker while still warm, mash with a ladle, adding milk, and set aside.
2 1/2 c jaggery, finely grated 2 1/2 c water	♦ Over low heat, dissolve the powdered jaggery in water. Turn the heat up to medium and continue to heat until the syrup thickens, stirring constantly to prevent burning. The final consistency should be that of a thin maple syrup. ♦ Add the rice-dal mixture and stir

Sakkarai Pongal - contd.

until well- blended over low heat for 3-5 minutes. Make sure the consistency is semi-liquid when fully blended, as the dish tends to solidify, when cooled.

4 cloves of cardamom, powdered
A pinch of saffron, soaked in 1 tbs of milk

- Add cardamom powder and saffron-milk mixture.

3 tbs ghee
1/4 c cashew nuts

- Brown cashews in hot ghee and add to the dish.

Note: If you like the fragrance to make a statement, increase the quantity of cardamom and saffron. You could also add a tbs of sultana raisins. Add them to the ghee when the cashews are nearly browned and leave them in for a few seconds before adding to the dish. A speciality dish made on Pongal day, a harvest festival , along with *Ven Pongal*, its savoury counterpart.

Badam Kheer

(Almond Payasam)

Ingredients	Method
20 almonds **or** 1 c slivered almonds, unsalted	Soak almonds in very hot water for half an hour.
	♦ Peel and grind to a smooth paste, adding enough water. If using slivered almonds, skip first step.
2 c water	♦ Add water to the paste in a saucepan and blend well.
	♦ Heat mixture over low heat, stirring occasionally, as it tends to boil over.
2 c thick, unskimmed milk	♦ Boil for 5-8 minutes before adding milk; bring mixture to a boil again.
1 1/2 - 2 c sugar	♦ Add sugar and simmer for 5 minutes.
1/2 tsp saffron soaked in 2 tbs of milk 3 to 4 pods cardamom, peeled and powdered	♦ Add saffron-milk mixture and cardamom.
	♦ Serve either chilled or hot.
4 -5 cashew nuts, chopped and browned in ghee (optional)	♦ Garnish with cashews. If desired, a few pieces of chopped pistachios may be added.

Semolina Kesari

Ingredients	Method
2 tbs cashews 2 tsp ghee	Using a heavy-bottomed pan, fry cashews to a golden brown in ghee. Set aside.
2 to 3 tbs ghee or melted butter 1 c semolina (rava)	♦ Add more ghee to the same pan; roast semolina for 5 minutes until the colour changes slightly and the roasted smell gets released.
2 1/2 cs water	♦ Meanwhile, bring water to a boil. ♦ Add boiling water slowly to the roasted rava (keep the heat on low), stirring all the time to avoid lumping. Allow to cook and thicken a little.
2 c sugar	♦ Add sugar and stir well until mixture thickens.
1/4 c ghee or melted butter 1/2 tsp saffron (soaked in 1 tbs milk) 1/2 tsp powdered cardamom	♦ Add saffron, cardamom and ghee, and stir until the ghee starts floating on top. ♦ Garnish with fried cashews.

If you have any questions, comments or suggestions, please email the editor at

info@aaranyapublishers.com

www.ingramcontent.com/pod-product-compliance
Ingram Content Group UK Ltd.
Pitfield, Milton Keynes, MK11 3LW, UK
UKHW041829200726
13854UKWH00002BA/900

9 780953 182718